A YEAR'S BIBLE COURSE

Based on the Scofield Reference Bible

By REV. CHARLES H. MORGAN, Ph.D.

52 Brief Lessons Covering a Year.
745 Review and Test Questions.
27 Chart Illustrations.
With Answers to the Questions.

NEW YORK
OXFORD UNIVERSITY PRESS

Printed in the United States of America

CONTENTS

CONTENTS

DESIGNS

Foreword

FOREWORD

Demand for Brief Bible Course. Our day is marked by the growth of large men's and women's Bible classes, in which a majority are busy people who will welcome a course having lessons only two pages in length. However, the Bible is a big book having a wonderful range of truth; and the publishers and the author of this course are convinced that it should rest back upon a Bible containing the fullest help that can be given Bible students in the compass of a single volume.

Based on the Scofield Reference Bible. The Scofield Reference Bible meets this requirement, and has a distinguished body of friends and lovers. This course, referring by page at every point to the fuller introductions and notes of Dr. C. I. Scofield, will enlarge the call for his monumental work. It gives in essence the main lines of Dr. Scofield's teaching of Bible truth, and refers students to the ampler statements in the Scofield Reference Bible itself. A foremost men's and women's Bible class teacher, himself a profound expositor of Scripture and holding in highest honour the Scofield Reference Bible, has carefully read every word of this course, and gives an unqualified verdict respecting its complete harmony with Dr. Scofield's thought.

A Full Year and Lesser Periods Covered. Seven main themes or subjects are here outlined, each covering seven or eight weeks or programs, the total of these being fifty-two, corresponding to the fifty-two weeks of a year. All of these subjects may be viewed as forming one year's full course, as they do not overlap. Should any pastor for his midweek devotional service, or any young people's or community class desire to cover from seven to eight up to fourteen or sixteen or twenty-one to twenty-four weeks, it is fully open to them to do so by combining two or three of the courses. Two courses that can be taken one after the other with the greatest unity of effect will be found to be Course I followed by Course VII, or Course II followed by Course III. Many other selections of dual courses can be made. For triple courses this order is suggested: Courses I, IV, VII; Courses IV, VI, VII; Courses II, III, V. Other combinations embracing four, five, or six Courses can be made so as to meet the needs of any situation or group. The full course of fifty-two programs or lessons would be an ideal one to use in the Home Department of Sunday schools; also in ministry to the shut-in, accompanied in each case by the Scofield Reference Bible.

Designs and Charts. Special attention is directed to the feature of designs and charts with which the Courses are enriched. This is an age in which, through moving pictures and the use of the pictorial everywhere, a premier appeal is made to the eye. The principle is adapted to these Courses, and from stage to stage, in the unfolding of the subjects considered, are found groups and clusters of ideas, and in other cases objects, arranged in forms to be easily assimilated, because the eye can at once catch their meaning and relations. As a similar aid to quick grasp of the material herein presented readers and students are asked to go carefully over the numerous boxed outlines and to note the side-heads with which the paragraphs begin.

Why These Seven Courses. Many other Courses might be laid out in the abundant wealth of truth and fact offered by the Scofield Reference Bible, but these particular Courses are arranged so that they may afford, as a first condition, a sufficient variety to meet the needs of all groups and classes. Glance at the Titles of the Courses on pages 3-4, and you will see that Course I is book by book and historical; Course II, historical and doctrinal; Course III, topical and pictorial; Course IV, biographical, doctrinal, and devotional; Course V, biographical and historio-prophetical;

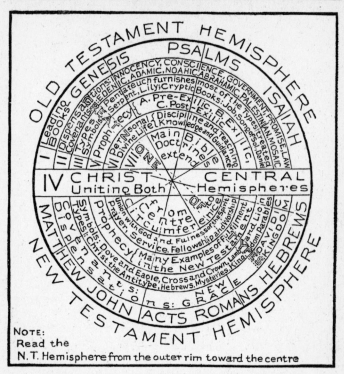

DESIGN A—COURSES COVER THE WHOLE SPHERE OF SCRIPTURE

Course VI, spiritual and practical; and Course VII, doctrinal. Choice can be made among these answering to the purpose, the preference, the previous training, and the personnel of a wide range of classes.

Covering the Sphere of Scripture. In Design A let us conceive the Old Testament as the germinal or opening hemisphere of Scripture, Christ as the central or equatorial factor or personality of Scripture, and the New Testament as the fulfilling or completing hemisphere of Scripture, and it becomes apparent that these Seven Courses cover or embrace in a surprising degree the whole sphere of Scripture.

Courses are Balanced and Two Hemisphered. As you study Design A, it becomes plain that each of the Seven Courses has the quality of being well balanced between the two hemispheres of the Old and New Testaments. In Course I the three big, weighty books of Genesis, Psalms, and Isaiah stand over against five important books of the New Testament. The several Dispensations of Man's early history are balanced with the wonderful Dispensation of Grace, which is yet to be followed by that of the Kingdom; and the numerous Covenants of the early age have as their counterpart the priceless and blood-bought New Covenant.

8

Great Zone of Types. The types treated in the Course given to Types and other themes are drawn chiefly from characters in the early part of the Pentateuch, from the tabernacle and its furniture, and from the things marking the priesthood and offerings. A great zone stretches across the Biblical field from the Pentateuch, through Christ, to the book of Hebrews in the completing hemisphere, where our Lord is shown as the antitype filling out all the larger meanings of the earlier ritual and service. The Symbols considered are traced through both hemispheres, as are the Mysteries and Cryptic Books.

Prophecy and Personal Divine Life. The extended and exalted table-land of Prophecy traversed in Course V, found and surveyed in the Old Testament, as represented by the first hemisphere, reaches its chief theatre of fulfilment in the second hemisphere. The seven phases of Personal Divine Life making up Course VI, and selected and unfolded especially for the quickening of the spiritual and personal life of the believer, receive illumination from the first hemisphere, from Christ, and from the second hemisphere.

Doctrines Pervade Whole Sphere. There is not a book of either the Old or New Testament to which or through which the lines of Bible Doctrines do not extend. It is very fitting that, according to the plan of Design A, the Scriptural doctrines should have their centre in the broad equatorial band assigned to Christ. One of the distinctive gains of recent times is that theology has become Christo-centric. The measure in which this idea is carried out in the Scofield Reference Bible is seen in the Panoramic View at the front, in which five great organizing ideas of the Scriptures—Preparation, Manifestation, Propagation, Explanation, Consummation—centre in the one theme of Christ, and in the fact that of the eight pages given to the Index, nearly one (page 1356) is required for the entries concerning Christ.

Christ Supreme. Course IV on Christ in the Scriptures is placed midway in the Seven Courses to indicate that He is supreme, and in Design A the broad central belt carrying this Course indicates His dominating place. Anticipations of His advent and work light up all the steps of revelation that go before; the dynamic influence of His ministry, sacrifice, and exaltation moulds all the development that follows after.

How to Form a Bible Class. While the Foreword speaks of mass classes, large numbers are not essential. An individual with a desire to know the Bible more intimately can gather a group numbering anywhere from three or five to ten or twenty people, and with the helps here provided can lay out and pursue a course of study to the mutual advantage of all. Let such classes meet in the homes of members, around the dining room table, or in a church or society committee room. Select a leader from the class or from outside as may seem best, but in every case a genuine lover of the Bible. Let the leader and, as far as may be, the members of the class, follow the suggestions that arise in this course out into the larger and richer field of the Scofield Reference Bible itself, and great increase in the knowledge of the Word of God will ensue.

Reaching Remote Sections. The very plainness and simplicity of this course should carry it into remote sections where there is often the greatest dearth of agencies that minister to the mind and heart and, at the same time, the keenest sense of soul hunger. In small hamlets and villages, in retired farm, mining, and mountain locations, having no church or Sunday school, there is need of some religious medium, some quickening guide which any thoughtful father or mother or any inquiring son or daughter can use. Therefore, A Year's Bible Course may become a pioneer teacher of divine truth in places where no other missionary voice has been heard.

Personal Self-Instruction. This Bible course is prepared on lines that cause it to be peculiarly responsive to methods of self-instruction. It brings the richest part—if we may so call it, the cream—of a remarkable body of Bible instruction within the grasp of the man or woman whose hours are filled to the brim with the daily task. Only brief minutes at morning or at night can be given to the soul's needs, but these suffice; and at the end of a year these persons through self-instruction can gain a good working knowledge of the Bible. The 27 Designs are their private tutors; the 745 Questions are their thoroughgoing and tactful examiners. Individual workers who do not belong to any community however small, who are not even members of a family—waitresses, nurses, sailors, chauffeurs, forest-fire watchers, lumber-jacks, plainsmen—can with these helps be Bible students.

Spiritual and Evangelistic Goal. Finally, A Year's Bible Course has a central and pervading purpose that means more than all else; for the course aims at the salvation and upbuilding of souls through the blood of Jesus Christ our divine Saviour. Dr. C. I. Scofield was not only a great evangelical teacher but a great evangelistic teacher. Multitudes have been drawn toward the gates of the life eternal, multitudes of converts have been grounded in the new life in Christ by the Scofield Reference Bible; and the author and publishers of this course press with prayerful aspiration toward the same goal. Evangelists and pastors can largely insure the spiritual health, happiness, and continuance of all persons newly enlisted for Christ by seeing that they possess the Scofield Reference Bible and this instructor in the same—A Year's Bible Course.

COURSE I
EIGHT LEADING BIBLE BOOKS

COURSE I

EIGHT LEADING BIBLE BOOKS

General View

DISTINCTION AND VARIETY

1. Genesis—patriarchal-legal.
2. Psalms—poetical.
3. Isaiah—prophetical.
4. Matthew—practical.
5. John—spiritual.
6. Acts—historical.
7. Romans—doctrinal.
8. Hebrews—antitypical.

Meaning of "Leading Books." While the eight books chosen for this Course are called "leading books," it should not be understood that they are sharply set apart from other important books, but that anyone who knows these eight books will grasp the sweep of the Scriptures. The United States has other big and important cities aside from those named below, but any person who in a through route should survey New York, Buffalo, Detroit, Chicago, Omaha, Denver, Salt Lake City, and San Francisco would realize the transcontinental sweep of the country.

Reach of the Course. When we traverse Course I, from Genesis to Hebrews, we are covering fairly well the whole reach of Scripture. It is not merely its extent in time that gives the Course significance, but still more the vast progression in thought—in revelation or unfolding of what the Bible was given to make known to man—the knowledge of God and the way of eternal life.

Old Testament Stages. The three books, Genesis, Psalms, Isaiah, represent three stages in the Old Testament revelation. Jesus indicates this when, as recorded in Luke 24. 16, he says: "All things must be fulfilled, which were written in the law of Moses, and in the prophets, and in the psalms, concerning me." Jesus uses the order of arrangement in the Hebrew Bible, and we the Christian or present order in the printing of the Old Testament, in which the Psalms and other poetical books come before the prophetical books. Note then that Genesis represents the stage of the law, Psalms represents poetry, and Isaiah represents prophecy.

Old Testament Progress. These stages represent progress in life and thought. The law is the first or primitive settling and ordering of life, covering the broad, every-day, universal duties and relations. The poetical books lift our thoughts and aims up far above the plane of laws and obedience to them, to the plane of experience, feeling, aspiration, and idealism. But we can see that this stage is concerned with the world within man rather than the actual world without. Such a book as Job does not take us through any course of outside history. We even find it hard to say in what historical period it should be placed. But the prophets are historical, and rise to a still higher range, where they seek to project the exalted ideals, noble standards, pure morals, and spiritual aspirations felt out in the poetical plane, and to make them live in the actual world of human society.

12

Gospel New Day. As the Course passes to the New Testament it presents the stage of the two Gospels, Matthew and John, in which the former, glancing backward, carefully traces how Christ answers to the utterances of the prophets, and the latter leads up to the full demonstration that Christ is the Son of God and eternal in His relations. Still onward goes the movement of life and thought in the last three books of the Course which may be viewed as giving the expansion of Christianity and its full understanding of itself.

The Church and the Holy Spirit. The book of Acts gives the founding and first steps in the upbuilding of the Church. It covers the advent and manifestation of the Holy Spirit, somewhat as the Gospels give the advent and manifestation of Christ. It thus rounds out the revelation of God as triune—the Bible revealing the Father in creation, the Son in redemption, and the Holy Spirit in administration. These last three books of Course I are therefore concerned with the final stage or plane of biblical revelation: Acts with this stage as history; Romans with it as doctrinal understanding; and Hebrews with it as eternal type or ideal.

DESIGN A—CHRONOLOGY OF THE EIGHT LEADING BIBLE BOOKS

Program 1

GENESIS

MAIN DIVISIONS. P. 3.[1]

I. Creation.
II. The Fall and Redemption.
III. The Diverse Seeds, Cain and Seth, to the Flood.
IV. From the Flood to Babel.
V. From the call of Abraham to the death of Joseph.

Genesis Period. According to the Ussher chronology appearing in the Scofield Reference Bible the period of time covered by Genesis is 2,315 years. P. 3. This is more than one third of all recorded time, as is shown in Design A, page 13, of these Courses, which also indicates the point or period in time of the material treated in the other seven Bible books making up Course I.

Book of Beginnings. Genesis is the opening book of the Scriptures and is recognized by Bible students as the book of beginnings. The beginnings of the heavens and the earth, of man and woman, and of all human institutions and relationships are indicated here, at least in germ or essence.

Creation. The first creative act, covering that of the heavens and the earth, refers to the dateless past, and gives scope for all the geologic ages. P. 3. It is proper to conclude that each creative "day" was a period of time marked off by a beginning and ending. P. 4. Genesis accords with science. P. 2.

Class Feature. A fitting topic for a short written paper is the names of God. Pp. 6, 7.

The Fall. The successive steps in the serpent's temptation of Eve were: (1) implied doubt of the divine benevolence, (2) adding to the word of God, (3) the first lie, (4) the appeal to pride. Eve fell into sin through pride; Adam took the step deliberately. Pp. 5, 8.

Redemption. The unfolding of God's purpose of redemption began in the statement concerning the seed of the woman: "It shall bruise thy head, and thou shalt bruise his heel" (Gen. 3. 16). P. 9.

Cain and Seth Lines. An earthly, material civilization developed through the line of Cain: a spiritual, worshipful progression originated with Seth. Pp. 11, 12. Extreme corruption of the antediluvian race occurred through the marriage of the Cainites with the Sethites.

From Flood to Babel. The judgment of the flood followed. Pp. 13–18. Again human arrogance uprears itself at Babel and God disperses the builders by confounding their language. Pp. 18, 19.

From Abraham to Joseph. The divine redemptive purpose then settles on the permanent agency of a chosen race, and its first unfoldings are delineated in the life and character of Abraham, Isaac, Jacob, and Joseph. Pp. 20–70. Design B shows the great movements of Genesis.

Genesis a "Law" Book. In several particulars we observe that Genesis is a part of the "Law," and that it opens the law books of the Old

---

[1] Figures following a sentence or paragraph and preceded by "P" or "Pp," designate pages in the Scofield Reference Bible.

Testament. As soon as man appears he finds himself subject to the will of God, which is the source of all law.

Obedience. We see here the race in its infancy and childhood, and in this stage the law aims at obedience, as the foundation with which all future right development must start.

Correction. In all our best modern methods in dealing with wrong-doing, we accept the principle that what is to be sought is not punishment, but correction. So Genesis steadily unfolds this principle that God's law is corrective. It firmly and faithfully corrects the faults which appear in order that it may secure true character.

Reward. Reward is inseparably wrapped up with all moral and spiritual growth and attainment, while, in genuine obedience to God's law or will, we grow unselfish. Genesis does not fail to start the race and the chosen people with these true elements of all law placed in clear view.

Questions

1. What are the five main divisions of Genesis? P. 3.
2. How do you explain the meaning of Jehovah as a name for God? P. 6.
3. In what way will you compare with this the meaning when the compound name Jehovah-Elohim is used? P. 6.
4. Of what two men is it written that they walked with God?
5. What two tendencies or movements disclose the corruption and waywardness of mankind?
6. By what means did God arrest these two movements?
7. What method did God then devise by which to work out His purpose of redemption?
8. What qualities did Abraham possess fitting him to be the founder of the chosen race?
9. What elements in Jacob made it possible for God to call him Israel?
10. What traits in Joseph mark him as one of the choice characters of the Bible?

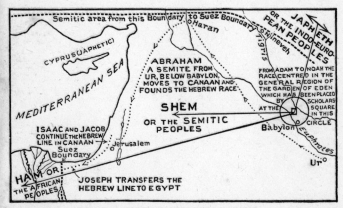

DESIGN B—LINES OF MOVEMENT IN GENESIS

Program 2

PSALMS

Key to the Psalms. The right approach to the Psalms is in this statement that they reveal truth "in the terms of human experience." P. 599. It is because the Psalms give us the reaction of the human soul to God under life's experiences that they continue to be so fresh and vital. There is no date to real human experience, and the Psalms minister to us to-day and will do so till the end of time. So wide is the range of experience given in the Psalms, and at so many points do some human experiences find expression in them, that only a few of the leading phases can be considered in this Program.

God's Favour. The first need of man, in the view of the Bible, is to come into God's favour out of his sense of sin and separation from God. When the right relation with God is attained there is an experience of good, of rest, of satisfaction, that crystallizes in the word "blessed." So the 32d Psalm opens with the words, "Blessed is he whose transgression is forgiven, whose sin is covered. Blessed is the man unto whom the Lord imputeth not iniquity." There appears here the great principle of imputation, and this statement is made, "Imputation is the act of God whereby He accounts righteousness to the believer in Christ, who has borne the believer's sins in vindication of the law." P. 1308. Then, in the 103d Psalm there are many aspects of the benefits coming to those who are in God's favour, and in connection with the 12th verse we find this note, "Three Hebrew words are translated forgive, forgiven . . . the fundamental Old Testament idea of forgiveness being not the remission of penalty, but the separation of the sinner from his sin." P. 649.

God's Word. Two Psalms, the 19th and the 119th, with particular fulness exalt the Word of God. Many can give from memory or should memorize verses 7 to 11 of the 19th Psalm. The 119th Psalm is distinguished as the longest, as alliterative, as having twenty-two sections of eight verses each with each verse of a section in the original beginning with successive letters of the Hebrew alphabet; and probably eight words for the Bible, such as law, commandment, precepts, testimony, originally found in each of the eight verses of each section. As Matthew Henry calls this Psalm "a chest of gold rings," we may call these eight terms for the Bible the jewels in the rings.

Class Feature. Members may state briefly what markings or memory devices help them to grasp Bible truth.

Uprightness, Devotion. In this life and experience the child of God should show balance. So, uprightness of walk, in Psalms 1 and 15, may be placed beside thirsting for more of God, in Psalms 42 and 43.

God's Presence. Psalm 3, a morning prayer, and Psalm 4, an evening prayer, together give the sense of God's daily presence round about His children. Psalm 121, often called the Traveller's Psalm, is one of the Psalms of ascent, "perhaps chanted by the people as they went up to Jerusalem to the feast," p. 662, and completes the assurance of God's presence whether we are at home or abroad.

God's Care and Help. The thread on which are strung many of the Psalms that are greatly endeared to us is our desire for God's care and help. Sometimes the Psalm writer rests so fully in the sense of this care that there results the 23rd or 37th Psalm; again there is tribulation but confident hope of help, as in Psalms 71 and 91; or, once more, there may be the pleading cry for deliverance of one overwhelmed with distress, as in Psalms 73 and 143.

Thankfulness and Praise. As the Psalms are "the inspired prayer and praise book of Israel," p. 599, it is found that recitals of God's goodness and summoning of all musical instruments and all elements of nature to join in God's praise have their place. Six such Psalms may be named: the joyous 34th and 107th; the stately 67th and Old Hundredth; and the glorious choral swing of the 148th and 150th. The chief Hebrew musical instruments are shown in Design C.

Questions

1. What is involved in finding God's favour?
2. How many different terms for the Bible can you find in the 119th Psalm?
3. Can you give three traits that characterize the upright man?
4. What comparison is used in showing the Psalmist's thirst for God?
5. For what feasts did the people go up to Jerusalem? P. 622.
6. In what verse are we enjoined to rest in the Lord?
7. What are some assurances of God's help in Psalm 91?
8. Can you give five points in the picture of "the prosperity of the wicked" in Psalm 73?
9. What four verses in Psalm 107 repeat the refrain asking praise for God's goodness?
10. What are five terms for musical instruments in Psalm 150?

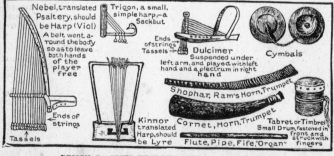

DESIGN C—CHIEF HEBREW MUSICAL INSTRUMENTS

Program 3

ISAIAH

Qualities. If one prophetical book is to be chosen as representative of all it will be Isaiah because of the great qualities of the prophet, and of his writings. "Isaiah is justly accounted chief of the writing prophets. He has the more comprehensive testimony and is distinctively the prophet of redemption. Nowhere else in the Scriptures written under the law have we so clear a view of grace." P. 713. We can picture him at the beginning as a young man of lofty mien, having the comprehensive grasp of a statesman as he looked out over the world of his time, while in his inner soul he listened to the voice of God.

Correction of Evils. In an age of contrast in social conditions, when monopolies of privilege and property led to displays of fashion and luxury much as in our own day, we see the prophet in the bold utterances of the first chapters. Pp. 714–717.

Class Feature. Let there be a short paper by a class member comparing the social conditions, as shown in Isaiah, chaps. 3-5, with those of to-day.

Transforming Vision. The vision of the glory of God in the temple at Jerusalem attended by the adoring seraphim, raised the spirit of Isaiah to a height of consecration before unattained. At the close he could say: "Here am I; send me." P. 718.

Immanuel. "The prophecy is not addressed to the faithless Ahaz, but to the whole 'house of David.' It was a continuing prophecy addressed to the Davidic family, and accounts at once for the instant assent of Mary (Lk. 1. 38)." P. 719.

Assyria and Other Kingdoms. In the central range of Isaiah the rising power of Assyria looms like a mountain. Lesser summits are Ethiopia, Egypt, Ephraim, and Judah. Pp. 720–743.

Coming and Overthrow of the Assyrians. One of the thrilling scenes of history is enacted when the Assyrian hosts that have shown themselves irresistible invade Judah and threaten Jerusalem. We see the insolence of the commander on the one side, and on the other the sublime faith

18

and the poise of Isaiah, the prayer of Hezekiah, and God's answer in the destruction of 185,000 of the invaders in one night. Pp. 743–746.

PART II. LOOKING BEYOND THE CAPTIVITIES. ISAIAH, CHAPS. 40–66.

The prophet's new message. P. 747.	Vicarious sacrifice of Christ. P. 760.
God's greatness: Man's weakness. Pp. 747–749.	The everlasting salvation. P. 761.
Christ, Servant of Jehovah. P. 750.	Ethical instructions. Pp. 762–764.
Prophecy concerning Cyrus. Pp. 753, 754.	Deliverer out of Zion. P. 765.
Judgment upon Babylon. P. 755.	Two Advents in one view. P. 766.
Israel cherished and restored. Pp. 756–758.	Day of vengeance. P. 767.
Jerusalem in the kingdom-age. Pp. 759–760.	Fear and hope of the remnant. P. 767.
	Answer of Jehovah in eternal blessing. Pp. 769–771.

God's All-Sufficient Greatness. The new message is one of tender yet profound assurance of God's power in nature and among the nations. He raises up Cyrus and quenches the effect of newly formed idols. His peoples are cherished and promised restoration, while Babylon is to be brought low. Pp. 747–758.

The Servant of Jehovah. The figure of Jehovah's servant appears; on the one hand, weak, rejected, offering himself as a vicarious sacrifice; on the other hand, a mighty conqueror, taking vengeance on the nations and restoring Israel. The two aspects reveal Christ in the first and the second advents. Pp. 750, 760, 766, 767.

Kingdom Blessing Pictured. At one point the prophet sketches Jerusalem in the kingdom-age. Pp. 759, 760. At the close the more complete picture is given. Pp. 769–771.

Questions

1. Why may Isaiah be accounted the chief of the writing prophets?
2. What are some of his qualities as a man?
3. Can you cite three pictures in the social state of Isaiah's time that resemble that of our own?
4. In what way did his vision in the temple develop him?
5. What great world power is a menace in the early part of Isaiah's prophecies?
6. Name the kings of Judah during the prophetic life of Isaiah?
7. Who was king when the Assyrian invasion came?
8. What controlling world kingdoms appear in the second part of Isaiah?
9. Which of these was led by Cyrus?
10. What chapter of Isaiah is most closely Messianic?

Program 4

MATTHEW

MAIN DIVISIONS. P. 993.

I. Christ's Manifestation to Israel as King and Rejection. Matt. 1. 1–25. 46.

II. His sacrifice and resurrection as Son of Abraham—yielding a Gospel for the whole world. Matt. 26. 1–28. 8.

III. Risen Lord in Ministry to His own. Matt. 28. 9–20.

Ministry of John the Baptist. Christ's forerunner said, "Repent ye; for the kingdom of heaven is at hand." The phrase, kingdom of heaven, is peculiar to Matthew and signifies the Messianic rule of Christ. It is called the kingdom of the heavens (literal meaning) because it is the rule of the heavens over the earth. P. 996.

Christ's Baptism. John's baptism was the voice of God to Israel, and the believing remnant responded. It was an act of righteousness on the part of Him who had become, as to the flesh, an Israelite, to take His place with the believing remnant. P. 997.

Christ's Temptation. Satan's one object in the threefold temptation was to induce Christ to act from Himself, in independency of His Father. P. 997.

Sermon on the Mount. The King, in Matt. 5–7, declares the *principles* of the kingdom. It gives the divine constitution for the righteous government of the earth, and transfers the offence from the overt act to the motive. There is a beautiful moral application to the Christian. These principles fundamentally reappear in the teaching of the Epistles. Pp. 999, 1,000.

Kingdom of God. The kingdom of God is universal, including all moral intelligences willingly subject to the will of God, while the kingdom of heaven is Messianic, mediatorial, and Davidic, and has for its object the establishment of the kingdom of God in the earth. Since the kingdom of heaven is the earthly sphere of the universal kingdom of God, the two have almost all things in common. The parables of the wheat and tares and of the net are not spoken of the kingdom of God. In that kingdom there are neither tares nor bad fish. P. 1003.

Apostles Chosen. The apostles were chosen directly by the Lord Himself, or, as in the case of Barnabas, by the Holy Spirit. They were endued with sign gifts, miraculous powers which were the divine credentials of their office. To one of them, Peter, were given the keys of the kingdom of heaven, viewed as the sphere of Christian profession. P. 1008.

Jesus Rejected, and His New Message. The places chosen for the testing of the nation, Chorazin, Bethsaida, etc., having rejected both John and Jesus, the rejected King now speaks of judgment. The final official rejection is later. (Matt. 27. 31-37.) The King now turns from the rejecting *nation* and offers, not the *kingdom*, but *rest* and *service* to such in the nation as are conscious of need. It is a pivotal point in the ministry of Jesus. P. 1011.

Anointing by Mary. Mary of Bethany, who alone of our Lord's disciples had comprehended His thrice repeated announcement of His com-

20

COURSE I, Program 4—Matthew

ing death and resurrection, invested the anointing with the deeper meaning of the preparation of His body for burying. Mary of Bethany was not among the women who went to the sepulchre with intent to embalm the body of Jesus. P. 1037.

Class Feature. Let some one prepare a short paper on the six Marys of the New Testament. P. 994.

Agony in the Garden. The value of the account of the agony in the Garden is in the evidence it affords that Christ knew fully what the agony of the cross would mean when His soul was made an offering for sin in the hiding of the Father's face. Knowing the cost to the utmost, He voluntarily paid it. P. 1038.

Results of Death and Resurrection. With the death and resurrection of Christ begins the "dispensation of the grace of God." Under grace God freely gives to the believing sinner eternal life; accounts to him a perfect righteousness; and accords to him a perfect position. P. 1044.

Questions

1. With what two Old Testament covenants does the Gospel of Matthew connect Christ? P. 993.
2. How many Marys can be distinguished in the New Testament? P. 994.
3. What is the meaning of the kingdom of heaven? P. 996.
4. How are we to define the kingdom of God as distinct from it? P. 1003.
5. Why was Jesus baptized? P. 997.
6. What was Satan's object in the threefold temptation of Christ? Pp. 997, 998.
7. What was Christ's aim in the Sermon on the Mount? Pp. 999, 1000.
8. What passages show the rejection of Jesus? P. 1011.
9. What experience on the cross is it thought Christ foresaw in the agony in the Garden?
10. What are the results of Christ's death and resurrection to the believing sinner? P. 1044.

Program 5

JOHN

Logos. In the Prologue, the word Logos, as a designation for Christ, is shown to be a peculiarly happy term, because in Him are embodied all the treasures of divine wisdom. He is from eternity, but especially in the incarnation, the expression of the thought of Deity. In Him Deity is told out. P. 1114.

Public Ministry. Near the opening of His ministry Jesus had the important interview with Nicodemus, in which He brought out the necessity of the new birth in view of the incapacity of the natural man to apprehend the kingdom of God. Even when gifted, moral, or refined, the natural man is blind to spiritual truth and unable to enter the kingdom. The new birth is not a reformation of the old nature, but a creative act of the Holy Spirit. Pp. 1115, 1117.

Christ as Shepherd. As the "Good" Shepherd He gives His life for the sheep. He is the "Great" Shepherd, as brought by resurrection again from the dead, to care for and make perfect the sheep. He is the "Chief" Shepherd, as coming in glory to give crowns of reward to the faithful shepherds. P. 1129.

Christ and Gentiles. In John the Gospel becomes most general, most free from Jewish limitations and assimilated to a world view. And at the close of the Public Ministry section we note that a company of Gentiles actually come saying: "We would see Jesus." Then it is stated: "For Gentiles the corn of wheat must fall into the ground and die; Christ must be lifted up on the cross and believed in as a sacrifice for sin." P. 1132.

Class Feature. Let there be a short paper on the Gospel and Christ's mission and ministry as related to Jews and Gentiles. Pp. 989, 1020, 1029, 1030, 1127, 1132.

Private Ministry to Christ's Own. The believer is cleansed as before the law from all sin "once for all," but needs ever to bring his daily sins to the Father in confession, that he may abide in unbroken fellowship with the Father and with the Son. The blood of Christ answers forever to all the law could say as to the believer's *guilt,* but he needs constant cleansing from the *defilement* of sin. P. 1134.

"Comforter" or "Advocate." The Greek *Parakletos,* meaning "one called alongside to help," is rendered in the Gospel of John as "Comforter," and in his first Epistle as "Advocate." Christ is the believer's Paraclete with the Father when he sins; and the Holy Spirit the believer's indwelling Paraclete to help his ignorance and infirmity, and to make intercession. P. 1136.

22

Deity of Christ. In all the Gospels alike is revealed one unique personality. Jesus is especially made manifest as God in John. P. 990. Christ's own affirmation of His Deity is most marked in John and is reenforced in the other Gospels. P. 1145.

Master of Service. In the Epilogue the risen Christ is shown as Master of our service. When Peter says, "I go a fishing," and the six others respond, "We also go with thee," we have the example of self-willed service under human leadership, with its barren result, for "That night they caught nothing"; and when Jesus asked them in the morning, "Children, have ye any meat?" they had to answer, "No." But Christ-directed service brings the result that one casting of the net lands a hundred and fifty-three big fish. Then the Master, after He had refreshed them, calls out the declaration of love as the acceptable motive of service. Pp. 1144–1146.

Questions

1. What is the meaning of Logos, translated "Word," in the Prologue of John's Gospel?
2. What especially does the Logos express in the incarnation?
3. What is the nature of the new birth?
4. Can you give two instances of Gentiles coming for help or enlightenment to Christ? Pp. 1005, 1020, 1132.
5. How does Christ adjust us to the guilt of sin and to its defilement?
6. What is the meaning of the Greek word *parakletos?*
7. By what two words do we know it?
8. What is the Godward and manward office of the Paraclete?
9. Under what term is Christ especially made manifest in the Fourth Gospel?
10. What are three assertions of Christ that uphold His Deity?

Program 6

ACTS

MAIN DIVISIONS. P. 1147.

Petrine Part, chaps. 1–9.
Pauline Part, chaps. 10–28.

Part I, Acts, Chaps. 1–9

Peter Prominent in Part I. In the first nine chapters of Acts, Peter is the prominent personage, Jerusalem is the centre around which the history of the beginning of the Christian church revolves, and during this stage the development is chiefly among the Jews. Fulfilling the declaration of Christ in the Gospels, Peter has the privilege of using the keys, to open the kingdom, considered as the sphere of profession, first, to the Jews at Pentecost, and, second, to the Gentiles in the house of Cornelius. P. 1147.

Advent of the Holy Spirit. After the resurrection-ministry of Christ and the restoring of the apostolic circle to twelve, there came, in response to the prayer of the company of believers, the outpouring or advent of the Holy Spirit at Pentecost. When Peter, as recorded in the tenth chapter of Acts, opened the door of the kingdom to the Gentiles, the Holy Spirit without delay or other condition than faith, was given to those who believed. This is the permanent fact for the entire church-age. P. 1149.

Peter as Apostle-Founder. Peter was fitted by his gifts and courage, after conversion, to be leader and spokesman among the original twelve apostles. Therefore he received "the keys," that is, the commission from Christ to inaugurate the Gospel movement among Jews and Gentiles. He was the first founder of the church, not the foundation, and other founders, and especially Paul, were to follow. There is in the Greek a play upon the words used by Christ to Peter, "thou art Peter [*petros*—literally, 'a little rock'], and upon this rock [*Petra*] I will build my church." Christ does not promise to build His church upon Peter, but upon Himself, as Peter himself is careful to tell us (1 Pet. 2. 4-9). P. 1021.

Class Feature. A brief canvass of the qualities of Peter and Paul that fitted each for his part in Acts.

Part II. Acts, Chaps. 10–28

Transition to Paul. The Petrine and the Pauline parts of Acts overlap or intermingle more or less through chapters nine to fifteen. Chapters eleven, twelve, and fifteen are also transitional in the sense that the development passes from the Jews to the Gentiles, from law to grace. In location also the centre changes from Jerusalem to Antioch in Syria, with Ephesus, Corinth, and Rome looming in the line of advance.

Paul Getting His Adjustment. Paul, fresh from the vision of the glory of Christ on the way to Damascus, puts the emphasis on Christ's Deity. He laboured in Damascus after his return from Arabia. He made visits to Jerusalem, where he conferred with Peter, and James, the Lord's brother, the leader of the Jewish section of the church, thus preventing as far as possible any division. P. 1161.

Paul's Great Ministry. Paul's wonderful course as a Christian apostle and leader is given in Acts, chapters 13–28, and covers his three missionary journeys; his arrest in Jerusalem and imprisonment for two years at Cæsarea; and his trials, appeal to Cæsar, voyage to Rome, and ministry there, though a prisoner. It has been much disputed whether he endured two Roman imprisonments; and the accepted view is that he had two such periods, with a year of release, travel, and ministry among the churches between them. Pp. 1166–1188.

Paul as Apostle-Founder. Christ commissioned Paul to be the chief apostle to the Gentiles. As the Gentiles, after the first few years, became and have ever since remained practically the entire constituency of the church, Paul thereby became, not the first in time, but the foremost founder of the church in all that means moulding power and authority. It was inevitable that a trained intellect like that of Paul must seek the underlying principles of the Gospel. The relation of the Gospel to the Law, and, in a lesser degree, to the great Jewish promises, needed clear adjustment, if Christianity was to be a reasonable faith, and not a mere dogma. In Arabia Paul sought and found that adjustment through revelation by the Spirit. Out of it came the doctrinal explanation of salvation by grace, through faith, wholly apart from the law, embodied in Galatians and Romans. P. 1189.

Questions

1. What two leaders determine the two Parts of Acts?
2. What people were chiefly reached by Peter?
3. What city was the centre during Part I?
4. What was the first scene in Peter's use of the power of the keys?
5. What was the scene of his second use of the keys?
6. Where was the chief centre when Paul became leader?
7. To what section of the race was his ministry chiefly?
8. Can you briefly outline Paul's course in his apostleship?
9. What are some of the things Paul did to avoid division in the church?
10. Did Paul have one or two Roman imprisonments?

Program 7

ROMANS

Through Paul Christian Understanding Is Given. To Paul was committed the unfolding of the doctrines of grace which were latent in the teachings of Christ. He originates nothing, but unfolds everything concerning the nature and purpose of the law; the ground and means of the believer's justification, sanctification, and glory; the meaning of the death of Christ, and the position, walk, expectation, and service of the Christian. Through him alone we know the nature, purpose, and form of organization of local churches, and the right conduct of such gatherings. This understanding comes out through Paul's thirteen Epistles, not counting Hebrews, and among these the chief one is Romans. P. 1189.

Great Words of Romans. The theme of Romans is "the Gospel of God," it being the very widest possible designation of the whole body of redemptive truth. P. 1191. Salvation is the great inclusive word of the Gospel, gathering into itself all the redemptive acts and processes. P. 1192.

Starts with Mankind as Guilty. All the world is found guilty, and a redemption is revealed as wide as the need, upon the alone condition of faith. P. 1191. Salvation is by grace through faith, and is a free gift wholly without works. The divine order is: first salvation, then works. P. 1192.

Redemption. The general meaning is deliverance by paying a price. The New Testament records the fulfilment of the Old Testament types and prophecies of redemption through the sacrifice of Christ. The completed truth is set forth in three words which are translated redemption: 1. *agorazo*, "to purchase in the market." The underlying thought is of a slave-market. The subjects of redemption are, moreover, under sentence of death, and the purchase price is the blood of the redeemer who dies in their stead; 2. *exagorazo*, "to buy out of the market." The redeemed are never again to be exposed to sale; 3. *lutroo*, "to loose," "to set free by paying a price." P. 1195.

Righteousness of God. The righteousness of God is neither an attribute of God, nor the changed character of the believer, but Christ Himself, who fully met in our stead and behalf every demand of the law, and who is, by the act of God called imputation, "made unto us . . . righteousness." The sinner establishes the law in its right use and honour by confessing his guilt, and acknowledging that by it he is justly condemned. Christ, on the sinner's behalf, establishes the law by enduring its penalty, death. There is no thought in propitiation of placating a vengeful God, but of doing right by His holy law and so making it possible for Him righteously to show mercy. Pp. 1194, 1195.

26

Strife of Two Natures. In the seventh chapter of Romans Paul represents the old Adamic nature and the new divine nature received through the new birth as striving with each other in him, and the second as suffering defeat; but in the eighth chapter he describes this struggle as having been taken up on the believer's behalf by the Holy Spirit, resulting in victory for the spiritual nature. He shows that the "law of the Spirit" has power to deliver from the law of sin which is in his members, and to clear his conscience from condemnation by the Mosaic law. Also the Spirit works in the yielded believer the very righteousness which the Mosaic law requires. Hitherto in Romans the Holy Spirit has been mentioned but once, but now in chapter eight He is mentioned nineteen times. Pp. 1200, 1201.

Class Feature. Assign to a member the preparing of a short paper showing what Paul means by Justification, p. 1195; and to another a paper on the meaning of Sanctification. P. 1353.

Place of Israel. In chapters nine to eleven, Paul shows that Israel's unbelief gives the opportunity for the Gentiles to be grafted into the good olive tree, Christ. But that the Christian now inherits the distinctive Jewish promises is not taught in Scripture. Israel as a nation always has its own place, and is yet to have its greatest exaltation as the earthly people of God. P. 1204.

Questions

1. Not counting Hebrews, how many Epistles are ascribed to Paul?
2. Which one may be considered the chief Epistle of Paul?
3. What does Paul make the church to be? P. 1189.
4. What are some of the great words or themes of Romans?
5. In what state does the Epistle at the start show mankind to be?
6. What three words or phrases do you choose as giving the meaning of sin? P. 1194.
7. What is justification?
8. What is sanctification?
9. What is meant by "righteousness of God"?
10. By what means does Paul show that we win victory over the old nature?

Program 8

HEBREWS

Writer and Date. The authorship of Hebrews has been in controversy from the earliest times. All agree that whether by Paul or another, the point of view is Pauline. No book of Scripture more fully authenticates itself as inspired. From internal evidence it is clear that Hebrews was written before the destruction of the Temple, A. D. 70. P. 1291.

Purpose. It was written with a twofold purpose. Its first aim was to confirm Jewish Christians by showing that Judaism had come to an end through the fulfilment by Christ of the whole purpose of the law. As a second object, the hortatory passages show that the writer had in view the danger ever present to Jewish professed believers of either lapsing back into Judaism or of pausing short of true faith in Jesus Christ. P. 1291.

Character. Hebrews shows that in Christ and His work God's revelation and process of salvation reach their final stage of eternal type or ideal. Such words as similitude, image, pattern, figure, example, shadow, like, after the order of, with the general meaning of *type*, and the word *eternal* occur again and again. The key word is "better." Hebrews is a series of contrasts between the good things of Judaism and the better things of Christ. Christ is "better" than angels, than Moses, than Joshua, than Aaron, and the New Covenant than the Mosaic Covenant. Not church truth directly, but the sphere of Christian profession is before the writer, and he repeatedly turns aside to exhortations needed to warn and alarm a mere professor. P. 1291.

Angels. The word angel is always used in the masculine gender, though sex in the human sense is never ascribed to angels. They are exceedingly numerous. Their power is inconceivable. Their place is about the throne of God. Their relation to the believer is that of "ministering spirits, sent forth to minister to them who shall be heirs of salvation," and this ministry has reference largely to the physical safety and well-being of believers. It would seem that this care for the heirs of salvation begins in infancy and continues through life. P. 1292.

The Rest of God. Christ is to us better than Moses the servant. The generation that came out of Egypt did not enter the Canaan-rest because of unbelief. But there is a better rest for the believer, of which God's creation-rest is the type. The believer rests in a perfect work of redemption, as God rested from a perfect work of creation. The believer is kept in perfect rest by mercy and grace, through the Son of God. Pp. 1293, 1294.

Our Great High Priest. Christ is a high priest after the order of Melchisedec as to *person, order* or *appointment,* and *duration.* In His *work* Christ follows the Aaronic pattern, the "shadow" of which Christ was the substance. Our High Priest within the veil assures our coming there too. Pp. 1294, 1295.

Christ as Our Sacrifice. By the law an order of priests was established who alone could offer sacrifices. Those sacrifices were "shadows" or types, expressing variously the guilt and need of the offerer in reference to God, and all pointing to Christ and fulfilled in Him. P. 1300.

The Believer-Priest. The believer-priest in his walk and worship has the example of Jesus, the chastening of the Father, and the warning of Esau. He does not come to Mount Sinai, but to Mount Zion and to spiritual and heavenly rewards and fellowships. He is to manifest separation and worship, sacrifice and obedience. Pp. 1303, 1304.

Class Feature. Let the leader direct the class in considering the state of believers in the interval between death and the resurrection. Physical death for the believer is called "sleep," because his body may be "awakened" at any moment. The soul and spirit live, independently of the death of the body, which is described as a "tabernacle" (tent), in which the "I" dwells, and which may be put off. At the believer's death he is "clothed upon" with a "house from heaven" pending the resurrection of the "earthly house," and is at once "with the Lord." P. 1299.

Questions

1. What can be said as to the authorship of Hebrews?
2. Before what event would you place the date?
3. What is the purpose of Hebrews?
4. What is the general character of the book?
5. What is its key-word?
6. How shall we describe angels?
7. What rest is now offered the believer?
8. After what order or pattern is our High Priest?
9. What was the significance of the Old Testament sacrifices?
10. How should we as believer-priests walk and worship?

NOTE ON METHOD OF EXAMINATION AND ESTIMATE OF STANDING

The review and test questions at the end of each sub-course and of A Year's Bible Course can be used by the leader of a class either verbally for review or for written examination or test of the members at the close of the course. For such a test the class should choose a period of an hour or two or an evening, all meeting together, in a home around the dining-room table, or in a room at the church. The leader should place the 25 questions on a blackboard or a large sheet of paper where all can read them, or otherwise furnish a set of them to each member, no copies of the text-book being used during the examination. The leader can take the test with the others if he desires to do so; and individuals not in a class can test themselves by seeing how many of the questions they can answer in writing without referring to the text-book while the examination is proceeding.

Each question correctly answered can count 4, at the ratio of 25 counting 100; and a mark of at least 60, or 15 questions correctly answered, may be considered enough to pass a person. The leader can determine the standing, or he can associate two members with himself, making a committee of three.

Bear in mind that in the 10 questions at the end of each Program the page references are to the Scofield Reference Bible; but that in these 25 Review and Test Questions at the end of each course, and in the 50 at the end of the book, the page references are to the matter of this text-book.

25 Review and Test Questions on Course I

1. What three Bible books represent the Old Testament, and what five the New Testament? P. 12.

2. What do Bible students call Genesis? P. 14.

3. Can you name five chief characters in Genesis? P. 14.

4. Why can Genesis be called a "law" book? Pp. 14, 15.

5. With what phase of human life are the Psalms largely concerned? P. 16.

6. What two Psalms very fully exalt the Word of God? P. 16.

7. Can you name some of the Hebrew musical instruments mentioned in the Psalms? P. 17, Design C.

8. How can you characterize Isaiah and the spirit of his prophecies? P. 18.

9. Can you briefly picture what occurred when the Assyrian forces threatened Jerusalem? Pp. 18, 19.

10. Who is the Servant of Jehovah, and how does Isaiah portray Him? P. 19.

11. What great discourse of Christ is given most fully in Matthew? P. 20.

12. Can you give three well-known Marys of the New Testament? Pp. 20, 21.

13. Which of the two kingdoms, "the kingdom of God" and "the kingdom of heaven," is concerned directly with the earth? P. 20.

14. What is the general meaning of the word "Logos" as used by John? P. 22.

15. What did a company of Gentiles say who wished to meet Christ? P. 22.

16. How do you explain the word "Comforter" as occurring in John? P. 22.

17. If the Gospels give the advent of Christ, what advent does the book of Acts give? P. 24.

18. Can you refer to some scenes which show that Peter is an apostle-founder of the church? P. 24.

19. What other facts and movements show that Paul is a church apostle-founder? P. 25.

20. Can you mention three terms that bring out some of the great doctrines in Romans? P. 26.

21. What two natures are shown by Paul as striving in us for mastery? P. 27.

22. In what chapter of Romans and through what Agent is victory made sure? P. 27.

23. What is the racial connection of the Christians to whom the book of Hebrews was written? P. 28.

24. Can you give some points showing that Christ's way of faith and life is better than that of Moses? P. 28.

25. What can you say about the priesthood of Christ and His offering as presented in Hebrews? P. 29.

COURSE II
DISPENSATIONS AND COVENANTS

COURSE II

DISPENSATIONS AND COVENANTS

General View

CONNECTION OF DISPENSATIONS AND COVENANTS

Dispensations. P. 5.	Covenants. Pp. 5, 6.

Linked with

1. Innocency........................	1. Edenic.
2. Conscience......................	2. Adamic.
3. Human Government...............	3. Noahic.
4. Promise............ 4. Abrahamic, and 6. Palestinian.	
5. Law...........................	5. Mosaic.
6. Grace..........................	8. New.
7. Kingdom.......................	7. Davidic.

Dispensation Defined. A Dispensation is a period of time during which man is tested in respect of obedience to some *specific* revelation of the will of God. Seven such Dispensations are distinguished in Scripture, and eight Covenants. Pp. 5, 6.

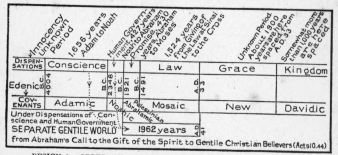

DESIGN A—ORDER AND PERIOD OF DISPENSATIONS AND COVENANTS

Names and Periods. The names for these are given above, and the period of each is shown in Design A.

It will be seen that they vary greatly in length, the Dispensation of Conscience, extending from Adam to Noah, being 1,656 years in length, while the next two, the Dispensation of Human Government, from Noah to Abraham, and that of Promise, from Abraham to Moses, are respectively 427 and 430 years. The Dispensations exhibit the majestic progressive order of the divine dealings of God with humanity, "the increasing purpose" which runs through and links together the ages, from the beginning of the life of man to the end in eternity. Introd., Item X.

Compared with Covenant. As compared with a Covenant, a Dispensation emphasizes more fully the divine side. God presents or dispenses a specific revelation or application of His will as the governing principle for each period, and when thus presented it tests man's response to God. But a Covenant involves the idea of an agreement between God and man, and may have reference to a particular individual or division of mankind. When we come to Abraham the succession of the Dispensations and Covenants apply exclusively to the chosen people until, under the Gospel, the Gentiles come in to be the spiritual Israel; and during that long period the Gentile world is under the Dispensations of Conscience and Human Government and the Adamic and Noahic Covenants. Pp. 19, 1013. See also Design A.

Terms Show Difference. A difference is shown in the terms used; those for Dispensations being chiefly broad and general in character, such as Innocency, Human Government, Law; while those for Covenants are in many cases derived from person or place, as Abrahamic, Mosaic, Palestinian. Yet, because God in the Dispensations presents tests, they may be temporary; and the Covenants, because they involve His pledged word, or agreement, in some manner go on forever. P. 20. In general, God deals with the race as a whole in the Dispensations, and with the responsive and obedient in the Covenants.

Analogy. As a means to a clear understanding of both Dispensation and Covenant we may take the analogy found in human partnership. The general laws or regulations governing partnership at different periods and among different peoples correspond to Dispensations. Some of these may go back to early times. There would be found similar yet gradually changing provisions concerning partnership in Roman, medieval, and modern English and American law, corresponding to the successive Dispensations. The particular arrangements and agreements of men in actual partnership under these laws would answer to the Covenants. Sometimes one party proposes the terms and the other party agrees to them; as in the Covenants, God presents the terms, and they are accepted by Adam, Abraham, or the chosen people. And, as men have often proved unfaithful to the partnerships into which they have entered, so the people have often been unfaithful to the Covenants into which they have entered with God.

Progress and Training. Both the Dispensations and the Covenants show God in a ministry to man that involves spiritual progress and training, with the final objective of benefiting the whole race. God's words to Abraham were: "I will make of thee a great nation, . . . and in thee shall all families of the earth be blessed." Man as a part of creation is to be delivered from bondage "into the glorious liberty of the children of God." If at first only one race, the Israelitish, is selected to be developed and trained, it is with the aim that Israel in the end shall transform the world. In these two series of steps, the Dispensations and Covenants, disclosing His mind, God begins with the simple and particular and concludes with the complex and universal. Pp. 9, 19.

Saving. But deeper than the purpose of unfolding and training man even morally and spiritually is God's design of saving man; and this is the final aim with which the Dispensations and Covenants are put forth and carried through. All the elect patriarchs, leaders, heroes, and heroines, saints, prophets, and apostles win their place because they serve to make effective the Dispensations and Covenants. The very Word of truth by which we are begotten to a new life is constructed on the framework of the Dispensations and Covenants. Grace and the Kingdom are inseparably linked with Christ, and the New Covenant is the New Covenant in His blood. And so the divine purpose reaches onward in the final Dispensation and Covenant unto the ages of the ages, to accomplish the utmost that is possible for the salvation and eternal glorification of the redeemed ones of God. Pp. 250, 1298, 1353.

DISPENSATION OF INNOCENCY AND EDENIC COVENANT

DISPENSATION OF INNOCENCY. P. 5.	EDENIC COVENANT. Pp. 5, 6.
1. Man created innocent.	1. Man to replenish the earth.
2. Placed in a perfect environment.	2. To subdue the earth.
3. Subjected to a simple test.	3. To have dominion over animals.
4. Warned of the consequence of disobedience.	4. To eat herbs and fruits.
5. Woman fell through pride.	5. To till and keep the garden.
6. Man fell deliberately.	6. To abstain from eating of the tree of knowledge of good and evil.
7. Dispensation ends in expulsion.	7. Penalty is death.

Parallelism or Correspondence. For the most part we find that the Covenants run parallel with the Dispensations. And in accordance with the analogy of human partnership we would expect the actual partnerships of men at a given period to be shaped largely by the laws of partnership of that period. Therefore it seems desirable throughout Course II to have each Program treat, along with a Dispensation, the corresponding Covenant or Covenants as nearly as this may be done. So, in this opening Program we consider the first Dispensation and the first Covenant, and it is clear that man's state of Innocency and his Edenic experience naturally belong together.

God as Creator. Elohim, the first of the three primary names of Deity, is a uni-plural noun, and in it the Trinity is latent. As meaning primarily the *Strong One* it is fitly used in the first chapter of Genesis, giving the creative work of God, of which the third step, after the creation of the heavens and the earth and of animal life, is the creation of man. P. 3

Man as Created. Man was made in the "image and likeness" of God. Man's innocency implies that there was at first the harmony of his faculties and powers, so that, in their workings, one was not set over against another; as the desires or affections over against the spiritual aims and ideals, and the senses over against the moral standards. The entrance of sin involves this opposition of one part of man's nature to another, producing disharmony rather than harmony.

Placed in a Right Environment. We have come to know how essential is proper environment to the continuance, vigour, and efficiency of every form of life. Whether it be some species of plant or some rare variety of animal life that is under examination, we assume that its survival is due to favourable environment. The fact that this is peculiarly the case with the infantile stage of the human species has been brought home to us by bitter experience, and accounts for the ever-growing attention given to the conditions surrounding infancy and childhood. In the stage of man's innocency, immediately following his creation, the race was practically in its infant and early childhood period, and God as the creative Parent saw to it that it had the peaceful, charming, and fostering environment that is the very essence of our idea of Edenic conditions. The setting was a beautiful garden, of tropic warmth and luxuriance, the animals were tame and docile, and served like the loved dog and cat of a baby to implant in Adam and Eve the first germs of social and benevolent sympathy.

Larger Testings. All animals, even the most intelligent, like the dog, the horse, or the elephant, continue to go through their little round of instinctive action, and the phenomenal training of one generation leaves scarcely a trace in the next. But for man there is boundless progression. Therefore God begins to lead man to walk with Him through the larger testings of the items of the Edenic Covenant, which each student of Course II should weigh with the utmost care, as displayed at the head of page 34.

Class Feature. Let a member in a five-minute paper draw out the larger meanings of these committals to primitive man, asking what their equivalents may be to-day.

Tragic Failure and Fall. The deeper moral testings of man, forming the heart of the first Dispensation and Covenant and designed to teach him obedience, resulted in a failure and fall that seems to gather to itself the gloom and mystery of all human failure from that day to this. Still, even now simple obedience is the lesson the race most needs to learn.

Questions

1. How many Dispensations are there?
2. How many Covenants are there?
3. What terms are used for the relation between the two?
4. What analogy makes this relation more clear?
5. What name is used for God as Creator?
6. In what consists chiefly man's likeness to God?
7. In what way is progress shown to be embodied in the Dispensations and Covenants?
8. To what extent is the training of man God's aim?
9. How fully is His purpose that of saving man?
10. What was the tragic result of God's effort to secure obedience?

Program 2

DISPENSATION OF CONSCIENCE AND ADAMIC COVENANT

DISPENSATION OF CONSCIENCE. P. 10.	ADAMIC COVENANT. P. 9.
1. Standard: the known will of God.	1. Serpent, Satan's tool, cursed.
2. Knowledge of good as obedience thereto.	2. First promise of a Redeemer.
3. Knowledge of evil as disobedience thereto.	3. Changed state of woman.
4. Conscience thus comes into action.	4. Earth cursed for man's sake.
5. Man placed under the Adamic Covenant.	5. Inevitable sorrow of life.
6. Again man fails in this second testing.	6. Burdensome labour.
7. The judgment of the Flood.	7. Physical death.

A Changed World. The change in the world of nature and of man as we pass from Program 1 to Program 2 is greater than any other which has been known. Then the outer world has all the quiet and attraction of an Eden. Thorns, poison, pain, bloodshed, cruelty, and death were unknown, or all their evil effects were countervailed. What we may call forms of physical evil have everywhere been present in our world from the moment the gateway to that first Paradise was barred. The innocency which attached to our first parents can scarcely be said to belong even to the babes of the new world into which they entered when they fell.

Good and Evil. Beginning with Dispensation 2 of this Course, we find ourselves in the mixed world of good and evil which is still with us. But let us note that, if, on the one hand, we have no longer innocency as the possession of mankind, we have, on the other hand, men and women who possess goodness or virtue, which is choosing the right or the will of God in the presence of the possible alternative choice of evil or disobedience to the divine will.

Framework Factors. This is a program of exceptional value because it embraces so completely the factors that are the framework of individual human life. Mankind organized and combined will be considered later, but the Bible from beginning to end is remarkable by reason of its exalting of personal life, and the second Dispensation and Covenant here treated give a striking array of the elements that mould the individual. Good and evil, right and wrong, compose the moral factor, which, next to religion, stands foremost, and has already been suggested.

Conscience. The very significant individual-forming factor of conscience gives name to this Dispensation and outfits man as a moral being, at once lifting him above the merely animal range where any true working of conscience is unknown. Conscience may be defined as the power or faculty in man by which he distinguishes between right and wrong in conduct and character, and which imperatively commands and obligates him to do the right and to abstain from doing the wrong. Man's struggle to secure permission to carry out the behests of conscience has created one of the battle-lines of the ages along which we may see Jeremiah, Socrates,

Stephen, Savonarola, Luther, and the New England Pilgrims as brave warriors. To acquire light from the Bible and other sources as to what is right is known as the education of the conscience, though perhaps more exactly the education of the moral judgment; conscience simply enforcing the decisions made by the judgment.

Religion. By the side of morals, or really before it, stands religion. Without its aid, man cannot be morally victorious, and in the Adamic Covenant we find the first promise of a Redeemer, while Satan, the arch foe, lurks behind the serpent.

The Family. The real unit of humanity is the family, and we do not find the Bible so individual that it leaves this factor out. In the changed state of woman is still preserved motherhood, though attended with peculiar anguish, and motherhood carries in its train parenthood, the family, and the home.

Labour. Another large factor that enters into the framework of normal human life is labour. We have reached the general conclusion that not labour itself is burdensome or oppressive, but only the conditions which man's ignorance, selfishness, or mismanagement imposes upon it.

Meaning of Obstacles. That the earth appears stubborn and slow of response to our effort, that it sets thorns and thistles in our path, that we must face inevitable sorrow and ultimate death, will convince us that we fight our way to success through obstacles. However, in doing this we win the greatest prizes of our earthly course—strength, true manhood and womanhood, meaningful personality, genuine character.

Class Feature. Let there be a short discussion on the subject of personal character and the means of its attainment.

Questions

1. At what point does a radical change occur in the life-history of humanity?
2. What factors then form the framework of personal life?
3. Can you give five or six words that are the pillars of morals?
4. Will you briefly define conscience?
5. What do we mean by education of the conscience?
6. In what promise does man's religious hope begin?
7. What cheering results may we see in woman's changed state because motherhood continues?
8. What good springs from labour?
9. How may labour be made burdensome?
10. What compensations can we win from obstacles overcome?

Program 3

DISPENSATION OF HUMAN GOVERNMENT AND NOAHIC COVENANT

DISPENSATION OF HUMAN GOVERNMENT. P. 16.	NOAHIC COVENANT. P. 16.
1. Man responsible to govern the world for God.	1. Man's relation to the earth confirmed.
2. The responsibility rested upon the whole race.	2. Order of nature confirmed.
3. The highest function the judicial taking of life.	3. Human government established.
4. All other governmental powers implied in that.	4. Earth secured against another judgment by water.
5. Both Israel and Gentiles governed for self, not God.	5. Ham an inferior and servile line.
6. Confusion of tongues ended racial test.	6. Shem the line of revelation and Christ.
7. Captivities ended the Jewish test.	7. Japheth the line of general civilization.

Beginning of Social Organization. Mankind is not to be compared to a circle with a single point as the centre, but to an ellipse, which is the form of the orbits of the planets, and has two points called foci. In the case of the orbit of our world, the sun occupies one of the two foci, and the arrangement is the same for the other planets. In the case of the orbit of humanity, from the creation up to Noah, one of the foci was occupied by individual man, and this factor was considered in the preceding Program. But in this Program we are to recognize that man socially organized takes his place in the other focus, so that we have the two foci filled with the individual and society. In any study or appraisal of mankind as a whole these two features, the individual and organized society, must receive almost equal attention, for both are vital.

Political Government. The first movement of man socially is the uniting of individuals or families in some type of clan, tribe, or state, that involves political government. Questions of the form of government, of its powers, of its laws, and of the penalities when its laws or regulations are broken have attended man through all his course from the time of Noah to the present. Probably there has never been such a variety of views concerning the form which political control should assume as that which prevails to-day.

Capital Punishment. The tendency to turn from capital punishment to life imprisonment as the penalty for murder and a few other extreme crimes is less marked than it was at the close of the nineteenth century. We seem to accept as final the decree given to Noah, believing that "by man shall his blood be shed," and that this judicial taking of life is the highest function of human government in the sense that in no other respect does social action so fully assume and represent the authority of God. P. 16.

Government Secular, Selfish, Divergent. Just as individual man failed in the first and second Dispensations, so social man or man in political government has failed in the third and later Dispensations even to this day. At once, in the period after Noah, general government showed such godless and secular ambition that the Supreme Ruler had to end the wild project at Babel by the confusion of tongues. As we trace the fortunes of the chosen people, we shall reach points in the future where first Israel and then Judah go into captivity because both are incorrigibly selfish and divergent from God's thoughts of true and right government. The awful misery and aftermath involved in the World War were not so much a disclosure of the failure of Christianity as of the failure of human government, so that God allowed the selfish and oppressive systems utterly to be broken in pieces.

Class Feature. Let a member present briefly the ideal of a government that would fully represent God's thought to-day, and follow it by discussion.

Races and Their Meaning. If it was made clear to Noah that his three sons were to be progenitors of racial lines that would stand out in history and that each would have its function and distinction we may be sure that similar points of distinction will be apparent in other races. Doubtless God can find a place in His age-long plans for the inherent endowments of each race, even as of each individual, whether these gifts be lowly or exalted. See Design B, Course I, page 15 of these Courses.

Hamitic Line. The lowly place of servitors to other races has been the lot of many along the Hamitic trail, as it winds in and out among the various eras and civilizations, but they have shown such qualities as have ennobled them. What greatness abides in cheerfulness, optimism, humour, laughter, and song in those who are facing hard tasks!

Semitic Line. A peculiar atmosphere or aura has surrounded and attended the Semitic peoples as they have demonstrated that the soul's power of contemplation, of turning the gaze inward in moral and spiritual self-knowledge, and upward in God-knowledge, has caused them to be the seed-bed of religions such as Judaism, Christianity, and Mohammedanism. All divine revelation is through Semitic men, and Christ, after the flesh, descends from Shem. P. 16.

Japhetic Line. The Japhetic line has been the chief creator of civilization through such contributions as have been made by some of the foremost peoples. We may associate Greece with poetry and sculpture, Rome with government and law, Germany with science and music, France with literature, painting, and other refined arts, Britain with commerce and colonization, America with constitutional freedom and idealism. But all must prove inadequate without the true religion of Christ. Pp. 11, 1342.

Questions

1. What aspect of man is placed beside individual man in this Program?
2. What do we mean by political government?
3. Is capital punishment to be retained or life imprisonment substituted?
4. For whom was man to govern the world?
5. What was God's form of punishment for the racial failure to govern unselfishly?
6. Which of the two kingdoms of Judah and Israel went into captivity first for governing selfishly?
7. What three racial lines were derived from the three sons of Noah?
8. How has the Hamitic line redeemed itself from the reproach of holding a servile place?
9. What is the peculiar privilege of the Semitic race?
10. What value attaches to the civilizing work of the Japhetic peoples?

DISPENSATION OF PROMISE AND ABRAHAMIC AND PALESTINIAN COVENANTS

DISPENSATION OF PROMISE. P. 20.	ABRAHAMIC COVENANT. P. 25.
1. It was wholly Israelitish.	1. Abraham's line to become a great nation.
2. Chosen people made heirs of promise.	2. He is blessed temporally and spiritually.
3. Every blessing by abiding in their own land.	3. His name made great.
4. In Egypt lost their blessings, but not their covenant.	4. He to be a blessing.
5. Dispensation ended when Israel rashly accepted the law.	5. Those blessing him blessed.
6. But law did not abrogate the covenant.	6. Those cursing him cursed.
	7. In him all the families of the earth blessed.
7. Law was an intermediate discipline till the seed should come.	

Marked Turning Point. As we enter Program 4 we pass an important turning point in the divine procedure. Hitherto the history has been that of the whole Adamic race. There has been neither Jew nor Gentile, all have been one in "the first man Adam." Henceforth, in the Scripture record, humanity must be thought of as a vast stream from which God, in the call of Abraham and the creation of the nation of Israel, has drawn off a slender rill, through which he may at last purify the great river itself. P. 19.

Promised Posterity. The covenant with Abraham begins with God's promise that he shall have a great posterity. This has had a threefold fulfilment. First, we note the natural posterity—"as the dust of the earth"—which may be applied to the Hebrew people. Next, we place the spiritual posterity—"look now toward heaven ... so shall thy seed be"—consisting of all men of faith, whether Jew or Gentile. In the third place, there is to be added the posterity through Ishmael. P. 25.

Hebrew Line Inaugurated. Abraham's natural descendants through the line of Isaac and Jacob now become the Hebrew or Israelitish race, destined to play one of the greatest rôles in human history. From B. C. 1918, the date of the call of Abraham, onward for almost exactly twenty centuries till the fall of Jerusalem A. D. 70, the Israelites or Jews, as they were later called from the province of Judea, were a political factor in the world's life. That is a very long period for any people to be of political consequence. Now, after the lapse of eighteen and a half more centuries, during which they have been a race without a country, they again have Palestine as a homeland.

People of God. However, it is not because of their wonderful continuance, their cohesion and separateness, their historical and general influence that the Hebrew people are to be studied, but because of the relation they have sustained to God. There were four objectives in God's development of the Israelitish race: 1. Israel was called to be a witness to the unity of God in the midst of universal idolatry; 2. to illustrate the blessedness of serving the true God; 3. to receive and preserve the divine revelation; and 4. to produce the Messiah. P. 19.

Class Feature. Let a member bring out in a short paper two inspiring suggestions concerning God's names: 1. that *Jehovah* (God known by His *redemption* name, as stated at page 6 of the Bible) calls Abraham (Gen. 12. 1), and 2. assures him by His name *El Shaddai* (Gen. 17. 1) (the *Nourisher, Satisfier,* or *All-sufficient One*) of His care.

Heirs of Promise. The Israelitish people became distinctively the heirs of promise. This insured to them the promised land. The descendants of Abraham had but to abide in their own land to inherit every blessing. P. 20. But note that the gift of the land is modified by prophecies of three dispossessions and restorations. Two of these have been accomplished. Israel is now in the third dispersion, from which she will be restored at the return of the Lord as King under the Davidic Covenant. P. 25.

Israel's Future Restoration. The Palestinian Covenant secures the final restoration and conversion of Israel. P. 1297. The exhibit of its items can properly be made at this point.

PALESTINIAN COVENANT. P. 250.

1. Dispersion for disobedience.
2. Future repentance of Israel while in the dispersion.
3. Return of the Lord.
4. Restoration to the land.
5. National conversion.
6. Judgment of Israel's oppressors.
7. National prosperity.

It is important to note that the nation has never yet taken the land under the unconditional Abrahamic Covenant, nor has it ever possessed the whole land. P. 250.

Great Evangelic Promise. The closing words of the Abrahamic Covenant, "In thee shall all the families of the earth be blessed," gives the great evangelic promise that is fulfilled in Christ as Abraham's Seed, and brings into greater definiteness the promise of the Adamic Covenant concerning the Seed of the woman. P. 25.

Questions

1. To what is the nation of Israel likened, when separated from the Gentile world?
2. For what purpose is this part drawn off from the great river of Gentile life?
3. What three lines of fulfilment may be noted as respects Abraham's promised posterity?
4. For how many centuries was the Israelitish race a factor in the ancient political world?
5. For how many centuries have the Jews been a people without a country?
6. What is their present prospect?
7. Can you select two chief objectives out of the four for which God called Israel?
8. How many dispossessions and restorations are the people of Israel to have?
9. What Covenant insures their final restoration and conversion? P. 1297.
10. What great evangelic promise is given at the close of the Abrahamic Covenant?

41

Program 5

DISPENSATION OF LAW AND MOSAIC COVENANT

DISPENSATION OF LAW. P. 94.	MOSAIC COVENANT. P. 95.
1. Man's state at the beginning.	1. Given to Israel.
2. His responsibility.	2. In three divisions, each essential
3. His failure.	to the others:
4. The divine judgment.	(1) Commandments.
	(2) Judgments.
	(3) Ordinances.

Point of Transition to the Law. The Dispensation of Promise ended when Israel rashly accepted the law (Ex. 19. 8). The Dispensation must be distinguished from the Covenant. The law did not abrogate the Abrahamic Covenant, but was an intermediate disciplinary dealing "till the Seed should come to whom the promise was made," namely, Christ (Gal. 3. 19). Pp. 20, 1244.

Grace Preceded as Well as Followed the Law. It is exceedingly important to observe 1. that Jehovah reminded the people that hitherto they had been the objects of His free grace; 2. that the law was not proposed as a means of life, but as a means by which Israel might become "a peculiar treasure" and a "kingdom of priests"; 3. that the law was not *imposed* until it had been *proposed* and voluntarily accepted. The Abrahamic (Gen. 15, 18, note) and New (Heb. 8. 8-12, note) Covenants minister salvation and assurance because they impose but one condition, namely, faith. That is, both these Covenants are on the basis of grace freely given by God, not by merit which man would vainly try to earn by obedience to law   P. 93

Extent of the Law Period. Law, as a method of the divine dealing with man, characterized the dispensation extending from the giving of the law to the death of Christ. It spans the period from Sinai to Calvary —from the Exodus to the Cross. The history of Israel in the wilderness and in the land is one long record of the violation of the law. The testing of the nation by the law ended in the judgment of the Captivities, but the dispensation itself ended at the Cross.   Pp. 94, 1244.

General and Christian View of the Law. In the Mosaic Covenant the first division of the law was composed of the Commandments, which express the righteous will of God. Pp. 95, 96. These give our general sense of the law. From the Christian point of view these are the right positions: 1. Law is in contrast with grace. Under the latter God bestows righteousness which, under law, He demands. 2. The law is in itself, holy, just, good, and spiritual. 3. Before the law the whole world is guilty, and the law is therefore of necessity a ministry of condemnation, death, and the divine curse. 4. Christ bore the curse of the law, and redeemed the believer both from the curse and from the dominion of the law. 5. Law neither justifies a sinner nor sanctifies a believer. 6. The believer is both dead to the law and redeemed from it, so that he is "not under the law but under grace." 7. Under the new covenant of grace the principle of obedience to the divine will is inwrought. So far is the life of the believer from the anarchy of self-will that he is "inlawed to Christ," and the new "law of Christ" is his delight, while, through the indwelling Spirit the righteousness of the law is fulfilled in him. Then in conclusion

42

ıt should be noted that the Commandments are used in the distinctively Christian Scriptures as an instruction in righteousness. Pp. 1244, 1245.

Class Feature. Let a member give his own experience and then draw out from the others how far the law of Christ is a delight and there is not servitude to the Commandments, but they are only guides.

The Judgments. The second division of the Mosaic Covenant, given in Exodus 21. 1–24. п, and called the judgments, is designed to govern the social life of Israel. Such subjects are covered as master and servant, injuries to the person, rights of property, and many of the more general social regulations. Following this the judgments touch upon such subjects as the seventh year of rest, the three national feasts, the conquest of Canaan, and preliminary steps in worship and approach to God. Pp. 95–100.

The Ordinances. The third division of the Mosaic Covenant, unfolded in Exodus 24. 12–31. 18, and termed the ordinances, aimed to govern the religious life of Israel. There is given the design of the tabernacle and its furniture, and the institution of the priesthood and the sacrifices. Pp. 95, 100–113. In general these reveal how the sin of the people can be covered. But the point is emphasized that the sacrifices did not directly "at-one" the sinner and God. An Israelite's offering implied confession of sin and of its due desert, death; and God "covered" his sin, in anticipation of *Christ's* sacrifice, which did, finally "put away" the sins "done aforetime in the forbearance of God." P. 110.

Questions

1. When did the Dispensation of Promise end and the Dispensation of the Law begin?
2. Was the Abrahamic Covenant abrogated at the same time? P. 20.
3. What great events bound the law period before and after? P. 94.
4. What are the three divisions of the Mosaic Covenant? P. 95
5. What do the Commandments express? P. 95.
6. What part of the life of Israel were the judgments intended to govern? P. 95.
7. Can you mention three things that the judgments sought to regulate? Pp. 96–99.
8. To what phase of the life of Israel did the ordinances apply? P. 95.
9. What agencies were created by the ordinances? Pp. 100–113.
10. By what means was the sin of an Israelite actually "covered"? P. 110.

Program 6

DISPENSATION OF GRACE AND NEW COVENANT

DISPENSATION OF GRACE. P. 1115.	NEW COVENANT. P. 1297.
1. Begins with death and resurrection of Christ. 2. The test is acceptance or rejection of Christ. 3. Good works as a fruit of salvation. 4. Ends with apostasy of the professing church and resultant apocalyptic judgments.	1. "Better" than the Mosaic Covenant as respects efficacy. 2. Established on better or more unconditional promises. 3. Obedience not from fear but from a willing heart and mind. 4. Personal revelation of the Lord to every believer.

Nature of Grace. Grace is "the kindness and love of God our Saviour toward man." Under law God demands righteousness from man; under grace He gives righteousness to man. P. 1115.

Twofold Manifestation. The first sphere of the manifestation of grace embraces the general realm of what we term Salvation. This is a great inclusive Gospel word, and covers such subjects as redemption, propitiation, and justification. Redemption is by sacrifice and by power; Christ paid the price, and the Holy Spirit makes deliverance actual in experience. The mercy-seat was sprinkled with atoning blood on the day of atonement in token that the righteous sentence of the law had been typically carried out, so that what must else have been a judgment-seat could righteously be a mercy-seat. Propitiation covers this process. In fulfilment of the type, Christ is Himself that which propitiates and the place of propitiation—the mercy-seat sprinkled with His own blood. God is propitiated; the sinner is reconciled. P. 1263. Justification originates in grace; is through the redemptive and propitiatory work of Christ, who has vindicated the law; is by faith, not works; and may be defined as the judicial act of God whereby He justly declares righteous one who believes on Christ. Pp. 1115, 1192, 1195.

Second Sphere of Manifestation. The second sphere of the manifestation of grace is in the walk and service of the saved. The weakest, most ignorant, and fallible believer has precisely the same relationships in grace as the most illustrious saint. All the after work of God in his behalf, the application of the word to walk and conscience, the divine chastenings, the ministry of the Spirit, the difficulties and trials of the path, and the final transformation at the appearing of Christ, have for their object to make the believer's character conform to his exalted position in Christ. He grows *in* grace, not into grace. Pp. 1115, 1211.

Works and Rewards. One of the divinely established principles in the Dispensation of Grace is that salvation is by grace through faith, that it is a free gift, and wholly without works in the sense that any work on our part is required or can in any way assist in securing salvation. The divine order is: first salvation, and then works. God in the New Testament Scriptures offers to the *lost* salvation, and for the faithful service of the *saved* bestows rewards. The two lines of passages are easily distinguished, by remembering that salvation is invariably spoken of as a free gift, while rewards are earned by works. A further distinction is that salvation is a present possession, while rewards are a future distinction, to be given at the coming of the Lord. P. 1214.

Class Feature. Let a leader or a member chosen call for special experiences of triumphs of grace, which may be voluntarily given.

Apostasy. The professing church is in danger of apostasy or "falling away." This is the act of professed Christians who deliberately reject revealed truth, such as the deity of Christ, salvation through Christ's atoning and redeeming sacrifice, and Christ's second coming. P. 1280.

Questions

1. Can you briefly define the nature of grace?
2. What are some of the more important subjects under the general idea of Salvation? P. 1192.
3. Among these how would you describe justification? P. 1195.
4. If the first sphere of the working of grace is salvation, what is the second sphere?
5. When a believer is given spiritual enablement, what is his part? P. 1222.
6. Does one grow into grace or in grace? P. 1211.
7. What is the right place of works as respects salvation? P. 1214.
8. How does one secure rewards? P. 1214.
9. Are they present or future? P. 1214.
10. Why is the New Covenant better than the Mosaic?

Program 7

DISPENSATION OF THE KINGDOM AND DAVIDIC COVENANT

DISPENSATION OF THE KINGDOM. P. 1250.	DAVIDIC COVENANT. P. 362.
1. Christ takes His kingdom.	Secures:
2. Closing judgment.	1. Davidic posterity.
3. Rest and reward.	2. Royal authority.
4. Glory.	3 Regnancy.
5. For Israel, restoration and conversion.	4. Perpetuity.
6. For Gentiles, smiting of image and setting up of kingdom of the heavens.	5. Immutability.
	6. Confirmed by Jehovah to David.
7. For creation, deliverance.	7. Renewed by Gabriel to Mary.

Alternate Terms. For the seventh and last Dispensation there can be used the alternate terms of "the Kingdom" and "the Fulness of Times." It is identical with the kingdom covenanted to David. Therefore the Davidic Covenant is ranged alongside the Dispensation of the Kingdom in this closing Program of Course II. P. 1250.

Recompense or Compensation. That God is a God of gracious recompense to His loving children is often exemplified in the Scriptures. So, in this instance, when David shows his desire to build God's house, the temple, God makes recompense by covenanting to build David's house, family line, or posterity, having royal authority or sphere of rule as a kingdom, and going on in perpetuity or for ever. P. 362

Class Feature. Let the leader call out experiences which may reveal God's method or law of compensation.

Covenant Confirmed. The eighty-ninth Psalm is at once the confirmation and exposition of this covenant of God with David. The covenant looks far beyond David and Solomon, since "higher than the kings of the earth" can only refer to Immanuel. P. 643.

Renewed to Mary. After the passing of many generations following God's confirming of the Davidic Covenant by an oath, it was renewed to Mary the mother of Jesus when the angel Gabriel said to her at the annunciation: "He shall be great, and shall be called the Son of the Highest: and the Lord God shall give unto Him the throne of His father David: and He shall reign over the house of Jacob for ever; and of His kingdom there shall be no end." P. 1071.

Opening of the Kingdom-age. The eleventh chapter of Isaiah gives the glorious picture of the kingdom-age, which constitutes the seventh Dispensation which we are now considering. It opens with a glance at the King's ancestry: "There shall come forth a rod out of the stem of Jesse, and a Branch shall grow out of his roots." P. 723.

Judgment, Rest and Reward, Glory. At the point where Christ takes His kingdom and assumes authority as its Divine Ruler other phases of the fulness of times occur which indicate the tremendous change and transition as respects Christ Himself and the saints as His Bride, associated with Him when He passes from the Dispensation of Grace and enters the Dispensation of the Kingdom. In the Dispensation of Grace, inaugurated by His own atoning death, sealed with acceptance by the Father in His resurrection, He continues in the state of humiliation as the seeking Saviour knocking at the door of human hearts and interceding for sinning saints that they may be restored. But at the Kingdom-age or Fulness of Times, both for Christ and His church, the time of testimony and divine forbearance ends in judgment; the time of toil and search for the wandering sheep ends in rest and reward; and the time of humiliation and suffering ends in glory. Pp. 1197, 1227, 1250, 1322, 1334.

Outcome for Jews, Gentiles, and Creation. For the Jewish people the kingdom-age holds in reserve restoration to Palestine and conversion to the Christian faith. For the Gentile world-system there is destruction by the Smiting Stone, accomplished by a sudden and irremediable blow, not by the gradual process of conversion and assimilation; and then, and not before, does the Stone become a mountain and fill "the whole earth." Finally, Christ brings into moral unity with God, and into eternal life, the new creation of which He is Lord and Head. Even the animal and material creation, cursed for man's sake, will experience deliverance. Pp. 901, 1198, 1206.

Revolted Province Restored. The King will restore the Davidic monarchy in His own person, establish His power over all the earth, and reign during the Millennium. The kingdom of heaven thus established has for its object the restoration of divine authority in the earth, which may be regarded as a revolted province of the great kingdom of God. When this is done the Son will deliver up the kingdom of heaven to "God, even the Father," that God—the triune God, Father, Son, and Holy Spirit— "may be all in all." Pp. 1227, 1341.

Questions

1. What two titles can be used for the Seventh Dispensation? P. 1251.
2. How did God recompense David for His desire to build the Temple?
3. In what Psalm is the covenant with David confirmed?
4. Where in the Gospels are found the words renewing the Davidic Covenant to Mary the mother of Jesus? P. 1071.
5. What chapter of Isaiah most fully outlines the kingdom-age? Pp. 723, 724.
6. Can you indicate the great change when Christ takes the kingdom?
7. What results come to the Jews in this new age?
8. What is the outcome for Gentiles?
9. What is the effect for creation?
10. In what way does Christ restore the earth as a revolted province? P. 1227.

25 Review and Test Questions on Course II
(For directions see Note on page 29)

1. What is the meaning of a Dispensation? P. 32.
2. Can you name three Dispensations that we know most about? P. 32.
3. What agreement among men resembles a Covenant between God and man? P. 33.
4. What two main objects has God in view in the Dispensations and the Covenants? P. 32.
5. What Covenant corresponds with the Dispensation of Innocency? P. 34.
6. When man was in a state of Innocency, how would his faculties and powers work? P. 34.
7. What kind of environment had the human race while it remained innocent? P. 34.
8. What makes the difference when we pass from mere innocence to goodness or virtue? P. 36.
9. What does conscience do in our life? Pp. 36, 37.
10. Can we see any good in the obstacles we meet with? P. 37.
11. What do we mean by society as the field of Human Government? P. 38.
12. What is one chief service of the Semitic race? P. 39.
13. What have Japhetic peoples contributed to the world? P. 39.
14. Who began the Hebrew, Israelitish, or Jewish race? P. 40.
15. What great objective has come in the line of this race? P. 40.
16. What recent fact may mean much for Israel's future? P. 40.
17. What great Bible personality is associated with the Law? P. 42.
18. What is the general period of the Dispensation of Law? P. 42.
19. If we as Christians are not servants of the Commandments, how still do they help us? Pp. 42, 43.
20. What is the meaning of grace? P. 44.
21. What Covenant goes along with the Dispensation of Grace? P. 44.
22. Can you give the general relations of grace, salvation, faith, and works? Pp. 44, 45.
23. Are we now in the Dispensation of the Kingdom or is it yet to come? Pp. 46, 47.
24. What Covenant belongs with the Dispensation of the Kingdom? P. 46.
25. Can you tell how this Covenant was renewed to Mary, the mother of Christ? P. 46.

COURSE III

TYPES, SYMBOLS, MYSTERIES, KINGDOM PARABLES, AND CRYPTIC BOOKS

COURSE III

TYPES, SYMBOLS, MYSTERIES, KINGDOM PARABLES, AND CRYPTIC BOOKS

General View

1. Early Character Types.	4. Selected Symbols.
2. The Tabernacle and Its Accompaniments.	5. Leading Mysteries.
	6. Kingdom Parables.
3. The Priesthood and Offerings.	7. Cryptic Books.

Key to Concealed Riches. A rich vein of Biblical truth and divine illumination runs through considerable sections of the Bible much as a vein of gold or silver may extend through long reaches of rock. It is a work of skill, understanding, and insight to discover and bring to light this treasure hidden from the eyes of many; and we shall find in this Course most valuable keys and methods that lie ready to our hand in the material that has been assayed to form the seven Programs. Perhaps no course will kindle a livelier curiosity nor better reward prolonged and loving meditation.

Clue that Gives Unity. The thread that gives unity to the several subjects is found in the observation that each of these themes first presents an outer envelope or body made up of men or things with which we are familiar, and then discloses a spiritual truth, conception, or message enshrined in or conveyed by this form. There is first the type, and then, as the real objective, the antitype; or we are impressed with the symbol that we may be led to know the value of the thing symbolized. The mysteries of revelation and of the divine purposes and procedure are shrouded in thick veils, that the final disclosure of what God plans for His children may be all the more entrancingly wonderful. Our Lord speaks in parables that the hostile and indifferent may be confounded and catch no meaning, and only the true-hearted be able to understand. The cryptic books of the Bible, like Job, Canticles, Daniel, and Revelation, are an offence and stumbling-block to the heady and self-sufficient, but very full of comfort and light to those who wait on the Lord.

Type Defined. A type is a divinely purposed illustration of some truth. It may be 1. a person; 2. an event; 3. a thing; 4. an institution; 5. a ceremonial. Types occur most frequently in the Pentateuch, but are found, more sparingly, elsewhere. The antitype, or fulfilment of the type, is found, usually, in the New Testament. P. 4.

Symbol Features. The symbols have, in Scripture, a meaning fixed by inspired usage. For example, leaven is the principle of corruption working subtly. It is invariably used in a bad sense, and is defined by our Lord as evil doctrine. Meal, on the contrary, was used in one of the sweet-savour offerings, and was food for the priests. P. 1016.

"Mystery" Scope. A "mystery" in Scripture is a previously hidden truth, now divinely revealed, but in which a supernatural element still remains despite the revelation. P. 1014.

Essence of a Parable. A parable is a similitude used to teach or enforce a truth. P. 975. In its outward form a parable is a short narrative respecting ordinary earthly things; and it is selected or arranged so as to

50

suggest comparison and, in case of the receptive, to impart spiritual truth. Christ's parables are at once marvels of literary beauty and instructive power.

Biblical Veiled Books. It has been shown that there is a principle in the parables which shuts their truth away from those who do not approach them in the right spirit. They act as a sieve and sift or separate the hearers or readers. They both reveal and veil the truth. So there are biblical books that have both this revealing and veiling or sifting power. The book of Job is to some degree a sifting book. How it sifted the characters that appear in it, as will be shown in Program 7 of this Course! Canticles or the Song of Solomon is another cryptic book that has this strange sifting power. Note these opening words in the treatment of this book: "Nowhere in Scripture does the unspiritual mind tread upon ground so mysterious and incomprehensible as in this book, while the saintliest men and women of the ages have found it a source of pure and exquisite delight. That the love of the divine Bridegroom should follow all the analogies of the marriage relation seems evil only to minds so ascetic that marital desire itself seems to them unholy." P. 705. In like manner it will become evident that Daniel in the Old Testament and Revelation in the New are among the most veiled, cryptic, and sifting books of the Bible.

Program 1

EARLY CHARACTER TYPES

Why Many Personal Types. It has been observed that the Pentateuch is rich in types. When it comes to the question of typical persons, this statement is fully borne out in Genesis, in which book there are more types composed of persons than are found in any other part of the Scriptures. If we ask why this is so, the answer may be that here is a law of spiritual selection. The operation of the Spirit and the intuitive path of revelation led to the choice for preservation for the guidance of coming ages of those characters that had in them this simple teaching power. These men and women embody in what they aim at and attain, or fail to realize, the race's struggle with sin, and its gravitation toward God and victory in Christ. Therefore the record of their lives can worthily make up the opening chapters of the Bible.

Adam. We find that Adam, the first man, of the earth earthy, is a contrasting type of Christ, who especially is lifted up by Paul in his great Epistles, like Romans and First Corinthians, as the second Adam, the antitype, and designated "the Lord from heaven." While the first man Adam was made a living soul, in other words, had life derived from another, that is, God, the last Adam was a life-giving spirit. So far from deriving life, He is Himself the fountain of life, and gives that life to others. Each is the head of a creation, and these also are in contrast: in Adam all die; in Christ all are to be made alive. The Adamic creation is flesh; the new creation is spirit. Pp. 12, 1197, 1198, 1226.

Eve. We next find that Eve is a type of the church as the bride of Christ. She, as taken from Adam's body, was truly "bone of his bones, and flesh of his flesh," but she was also his wife, united to him in a relation which makes of "twain . . . one flesh," and so a clear type of the church as a bride of Christ. Pp. 8, 1255.

Cain. Here we have a type of the mere man of the earth. Cain's religion was destitute of any adequate sense of sin, or need of atonement. P. 10.

Abel. By contrast we find in Abel a type of the spiritual man. He brought as an offering to God "of the firstlings of his flock." A lamb fitly symbolizes the unresisting innocence and harmlessness of the Lord Jesus. Abel's sacrifice was therefore at once his confession of sin and expression of his faith in the interposition of a substitute, and proclaims in the very infancy of the race the primal truth that "without shedding of blood is no remission." P. 10.

Enoch. Special significance attaches to the fact that the patriarch was "translated that he should not see death." He becomes a type of the saints who will be "caught up" before the great tribulation. P. 13.

Abraham. Viewing Abraham typically we first see him as contrasted with Lot. The younger man "chose him all the plain of Jordan" for present advantage; while the patriarch "looked for a city which hath foundations." The men remain types of the worldly and the spiritual believer. P. 30. But in a way that more fully brings out his greatness of character Abraham becomes a type of God the Father, who "spared not his own Son, but delivered him up for us all." P. 33.

Isaac. We note that Isaac is typical in a fourfold way; first, of the church as composed of the spiritual children of Abraham; second, of Christ as the Son "obedient unto death;" third, of Christ as the Bridegroom of a called-out bride; fourth, of the new nature of the believer as "born after the Spirit." P. 31.

Jacob. In his sojourn at Haran Jacob becomes a striking illustration, if not type, of the nation descended from him in its present long dispersion. Like Israel he was: first, out of the place of blessing; second, without an altar; third, gained an evil name; fourth, but was under the covenant care of Jehovah and was ultimately brought back. P. 43.

Joseph. While it is nowhere asserted that Joseph was a type of Christ, the analogies are too numerous to be accidental. First, both were especial objects of a father's love; second, both were hated by their brethren; third, the superior claims of both were rejected by their brethren; fourth, the brethren of both conspired against them to slay them; fifth, Joseph was in intent and figure slain by his brethren, as was Christ; sixth, each became a blessing among the Gentiles, and gained a Gentile bride; seventh, as Joseph reconciled his brethren to himself, and afterward exalted them, so will it be with Christ and His Jewish brethren. P. 53.

Benjamin. We see that Benjamin, "son of sorrow" to his mother, but "son of my right hand" to his father, becomes a double type of Christ. As Ben-oni he was the suffering One because of whom a sword pierced his mother's heart; as Benjamin, head of the warrior tribe, firmly joined to Judah, the kingly tribe, he becomes a type of the victorious One. It is noteworthy that Benjamin was especially honoured among the Gentiles. P. 51.

Class Feature. Let there be a discussion directed by the leader as to why Genesis is rich beyond other books in typical characters.

Questions

1. What part of the Bible is especially rich in types?
2. What book has many typical characters?
3. Of whom is Adam a type?
4. Of what is Eve a type?
5. What character is suggested by Cain?
6. By Abel?
7. Who are typified by Enoch?
8. By Abraham and Isaac?
9. By Jacob?
10. By Joseph?

Program 2

THE TABERNACLE AND ITS ACCOMPANIMENTS

Typical in Three Ways. The tabernacle, speaking comprehensively, is explained in the New Testament as typical in three ways. It is a type: first, of the Church as a habitation of God through the Spirit; second, of the believer; third, as a figure of the things in the heavens. P. 103.

Materials and Colours. The typical meanings of the materials and colours of the tabernacle are believed to be as follows: gold, divine glory; silver, redemption; brass, judgment, as in the brazen altar and the serpent of brass; blue, heavenly in nature or origin; purple, royalty; scarlet, sacrifice. Acacia wood, a desert growth, is a fitting type of Christ in His humanity as "a root out of dry ground"; the covering, gold, typifying deity in manifestation, the two the union in Him of deity and humanity. Pp. 100–104.

Divine and Human Order. In *revelation*, God begins from Himself, working outward toward man; while, in *approach* the worshipper begins from himself, moving toward God dwelling in the holy of holies. The same order is seen in the Levitical service. In *approach* man begins at the brazen altar, type of the cross, where, in the fire of judgment, atonement is made, and moves inward to the holy of holies and the ark or mercy-seat where he is accepted of God. Christ enacted this order in His last night with His disciples, as appears to be recorded in the closing chapters of John's Gospel, where the approach begins with the indication in chapter twelve of Christ's sacrificial death upon the cross, as if the company were at the brazen altar of burnt offering. Then His washing of the disciples' feet corresponds to the station at the laver. Next they experience the fellowship and high communion of Spirit that belongs with the symbolism of the holy place, with its sevenfold light, its showbread, and its altar of incense. This takes us through chapters fourteen to sixteen of the Fourth Gospel. Lastly, chapter seventeen reveals Christ offering His high-priestly prayer, as if He had entered the holy of holies and approached the mercy-seat. Pp. 101, 1133.

Ark and Mercy-Seat. Starting now with the ark, and taking the direction of revelation, outward from God to man, we proceed to note the series of types that are presented. The ark was located in the holy of holies, probably centrally, as indicated in Design A. It was a chest of acacia wood enriched with gold which also formed the mercy-seat with two overshadowing cherubim. Within the ark were the tables of the law, a jar of manna, and Aaron's rod that budded. In its use the ark, especially the mercy-seat, was a type of God's throne. That it was, to the sinning Israelite, a throne of grace and not of judgment was due to the mercy-seat sprinkled with the blood of atonement. P. 101.

Altar of Incense. Leaving the holy of holies and passing through the veil we find next to it, in the holy place, the altar of incense, typical of Christ our intercessor, through whom our own prayers and praises ascend to God. Pp. 110, 111.

Showbread. This consisted of twelve loaves, freshly renewed each Sabbath day, and arranged in two rows upon the table of showbread located midway on the north side of the holy place. The showbread typified Christ as the Bread of God, life-sustaining as the manna was life-giving, as the "corn of wheat" ground in the mill of suffering and brought into the fire of judgment. Pp. 102, 158.

Candlestick. The golden candlestick or lampstand, with its central shaft and six curved branches supporting seven lamps, was located mid-

54

way on the south side of the holy place, and was a type of Christ our light, shining in the power of the seven-fold Spirit. Natural light was excluded from the tabernacle. P. 102.

Class Feature. Let four members give respectively the typical meaning of the laver as Christ cleansing us from defilement, p. 111; the altar of burnt offering, type of the Cross, and which, being double the height of the mercy-seat, shows that the atonement more than saves *us*—it glorifies God, p. 104; the boards united by the "middle bar," representing both the one life and the one Spirit, p. 103; and the hangings screening off the court, their fine linen standing for that measure of righteousness which God demands. They bar out equally the self-righteous man and the open sinner, for the height was above eight feet, pp. 104, 105.

Questions

1. In what three ways is the tabernacle typical?

2. What is the meaning of gold, silver, and brass?

3. Of blue, purple, and scarlet?

4. What is the divine order of *revelation?*

5 The human order of *approach?*

6. What is the typical meaning of the ark?

7. Of the altar of incense?

8. Of the showbread?

9. Of the candlestick?

10. Of the altar of burnt offering?

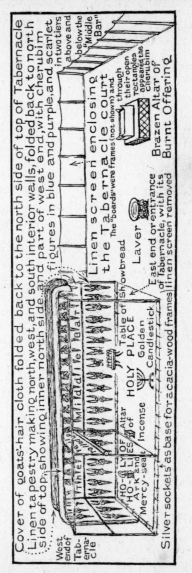

DESIGN A—OUTLINE OF TABERNACLE AND ACCOMPANIMENTS

Program 3

THE PRIESTHOOD AND THE OFFERINGS

King Priest and High Priest. Melchisedec was the type of Christ as King Priest. "After the order of Melchisedec" refers to the royal *authority* and unending *duration* of Christ's high priesthood. Pp. 23, 1295. He is a priest after the *order* of Melchisedec, but in His *work* He follows the Aaronic pattern. Pp. 106, 1295. For the clothing of Aaron and the high priest for highest ministration, see p. 108 and Design B.

Incense, composed of stacte, onycha, galbanum, and frankincense, a species of myrrh, compounded, and in its vessel

Odourous smoke of burning incense

Golden crown forming top of altar

Horn at altar corner

Altar of acacia wood

Staves for carrying altar of incense

Linen mitre or high priest's headdress, with "Holiness to the Lord" on front gold plate.

Onyx shoulder clasp, with names of tribes.

Urim and Thummim or breastplate of twelve precious stones.

Uppermost garment, with girdle, the ephod, of gold, blue, purple, and scarlet.

Next under garment, the robe of the ephod, blue, with bells and pomegranates on the lower edge or hem.

Undermost garment, the long coat of linen worn next the body

DESIGN B—HIGH PRIEST AND INCENSE OFFERING

Animals for sacrifice. The creatures acceptable for sacrifice are five: 1. The bullock or ox, typifies Christ, as the patient and enduring Servant, "obedient unto death." 2. The sheep, or lamb, typifies Christ in unresisting self-surrender to the death of the cross. 3. The goat typified the sinner and, when used sacrificially, Christ, as "numbered with the transgressors." 4. and 5. The turtle dove and the young pigeon are naturally symbols of mourning innocency, and are associated with poverty. P. 126.

Fire. Fire is essentially a symbol of God's holiness. As such it expresses God in three ways: first, in judgment upon that which His holiness utterly condemns; second, in manifestation of Himself, and of that which He approves; third, in purification. Accordingly, as operative in connection with the offerings, the fire which only manifests the sweet savour of the burnt-meal and peace-offerings, wholly consumes the sin-offering. P. 127.

Christ's Atoning Work. As interpreted by the Old Testament sacrificial types, Christ's offering of Himself has these elements: first it is substitutionary—the offering takes the offerer's place in death; second, the law is not evaded but honoured—every sacrificial death was an execution of the sentence of the law; third, the sinlessness of Him who bore our sins is expressed in every animal sacrifice—it must be without blemish; fourth, the effect of the atoning work of Christ is typified, on the one hand, in the promises, "it shall be forgiven him," and, on the other, in the peace-offering, the expression of fellowship—the highest privilege of the saint. Pp. 147, 148.

The Cross the Real Atonement. It was the cross, not the Levitical sacrifices, which made "at-one-ment," although that word is used where the word "cover" is the literal meaning. The Old Testament sacrifices enabled God to go on with a guilty people because they typified the cross. To the offerer they were the confession of his desert of death, and the expression of his faith; to God they were the "shadows" of which Christ was the reality. P. 148.

Class Feature. Let a member, in a five-minute paper or talk, present the subject of fire as a symbol or expression of God, and show its present applications.

Questions

1. Can you tell in what respects Melchisedek was a type of Christ?
2. At what point does Aaron become the type?
3. What engraved words were attached to the mitre of the high priest?
4. How were the onyx clasps on his shoulders engraved? P. 106.
5. What was his uppermost garment?
6. What was his next undergarment?
7. What was his undermost garment? P. 108.
8. What are the five animals for sacrifice?
9. In what three symbolic ways is fire an expression of God?
10. To what belongs the real power of atonement typified in offerings and sacrifices? P. 148.

Program 4

SELECTED SYMBOLS

Relation of Type and Symbol. As we now pass from the consideration of biblical types to give this Program to the study of the symbols of Scripture, we may first note the points of connection between these two things. It is plain that there is close connection, for in the matter relating to types we often meet with a sentence like this: "The inner veil, type of Christ's human body." This veil was the most expressive symbol of the truth that "by the deeds of the law shall no flesh be justified." P. 104. Here the veil is called both a type and a symbol. But we observe that it is counted a type of a "body," but a symbol of a "truth." As a rule we shall find that the typical meaning or expression of a thing takes us over to something else—the antitype—that is also concrete; so that the sun typifies Christ, the moon the church. P. 4. But this is not always so, for often we have a case like this: "The fine linen commonly typifies personal righteousness." P. 104. There is an emblematic or resemblance element in the type that is not always so evident in the symbol, which may be selected to represent an object or quality much as a letter represents a sound, whether there is any resemblance or not. When it comes to the verbal form, to say that "gold typifies Deity in manifestation," and "silver symbolizes redemption," p. 103, is to indicate that one word or the other can be used perhaps simply to give variety to the expression. But with this endeavour to clarify these two terms, we commit the distinction to the consideration of the class.

Class Feature. Let the leader draw out the members in a brief discussion as to their thought bearing on the respective spheres belonging to type and to symbol in the Bible.

Serpent and Lily. We treat the selected symbols in pairs, as it may be most illuminating to place one over against another. In the case of the serpent and the lily we may emphasize this contrast: The serpent, indwelt by Satan, so that man's enemy appears "as an angel of light," discloses evil as invading a world where innocence reigns. On the other hand we find the bridegroom declaring of himself: "I am the rose of Sharon, and the lily of the valley." P. 705. He also compares the bride to "the lily among thorns," p. 706, symbol of purity given the place of honour in a realm which mankind seems perversely bound to fill with suggestions of carnality and defilement.

Dove and Eagle. In the same book of Canticles we have the bride seen in Christ as "My dove." In herself most faulty; in Him "blameless and harmless," the very character of the dove. P. 706. But when Christ says: "Wheresoever the carcase is, there will the eagles be gathered together," and we learn that the griffon-vulture, often seen soaring in Palestine, is the bird referred to, we are revolted by the picture and symbol of decay and rapacity. P. 1034. The true eagle has from early times been the symbol of St. John or of the Fourth Gospel. See Design C.

Cross and Crown. The cross as meaning the sacrifice of Christ, is probably the world's most glorious symbol. The connected cross and crown rather pertain to the believer, as the symbols of his struggle and final victory. Matt. 10. 38; 1 Pet. 5. 4.

Lamb and Lion. The two symbols of the lamb and the lion are applied to Christ in the book of Revelation. He appears in the character of "a Lamb as it had been slain" (Rev. 5. 6), being the only personality worthy and able to open the book of redemption; and as He comes forth to answer to the challenge of this immeasurable need of mankind, He is proclaimed as the Lion of the tribe of Judah. Rev. 5. 5, 6. The two symbols belong to Christ in the first and second advents.

Questions

1. What shows the close connection between type and symbol?
2. How, then, are the two distinguished?
3. Why is it well to consider the eight selected symbols in pairs?
4. Under what circumstances does the symbol of the serpent appear?
5. Under what the lily?
6. In what connection is there introduced the symbol of the dove?
7. By whom and for what is there reference to the eagles or the griffon-vultures? and of what has the true eagle been made a symbol?
8. Can you make distinct the two uses of the symbol of the cross?
9. What is the application of the symbol of the crown?
10. Where and for whom are the two symbols of the lamb and the lion used?

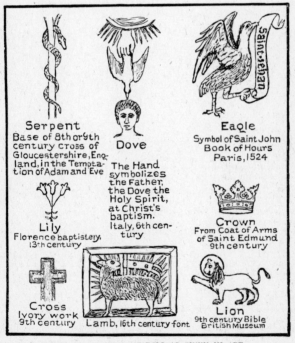

DESIGN C—BIBLE SYMBOLS AS GIVEN IN ART

Program 5

LEADING MYSTERIES

Reason for the Name. It is because the truths involved are only in part revealed that these specific subjects are called mysteries. They answer to the meaning of the term, and it is, moreover, a title given them in the Bible itself, rather than one imposed by scholarly study from without. It is at the point in Matthew where the kingdom parables begin that a list of the leading mysteries appears. P. 1014. The first noted are the mysteries of the kingdom, and these will be considered in Program 6, on the Kingdom Parables. The other chief mysteries will now be surveyed.

Israel's Blindness. The eleventh chapter of Romans shows that Israel has not irrevocably been set aside. The salvation of Paul proves that there is still a remnant, and the doctrine of the remnant also proves it. Israel's blindness and unbelief is the Gentile opportunity. While it is true that Israel is judicially broken off from Christ, the good olive tree, they are to be grafted in again. The promised Deliverer will come out of Zion, their blindness will pass away, and the nation will be saved. P. 1204.

Translation of Living Saints. The "first resurrection," that "unto life," will occur at the second coming of Christ, the saints of the Old Testament and the church ages meeting Him in the air; while the martyrs of the tribulation, which precedes His second advent, will be raised at the end of that period of trial, as a part of the first resurrection. The resurrection body will be incorruptible, glorious, powerful, and spiritual. The bodies of living believers will, at the same time, be instantaneously changed and will become identical in nature with the bodies of those that have been raised, thus reaching the same goal without passing through death. Theirs is the glorious mystery of translation. P. 1228.

Jew and Gentile Made One Body. That the Gentiles were to be saved was no mystery. The mystery "hid in God" was the divine purpose to make of Jew and Gentile a wholly new thing—"the church"—as Christ's body, formed by the baptism with the Holy Spirit, and in which the distinctions of race disappear. The revelation of this mystery, which was foretold but not explained by Christ, was committed to Paul. P. 1252.

The Bride of Christ. Christ's love-work for the church is threefold: past, present and future: first, the love whereby He gave Himself to redeem the church; second, the love whereby He is sanctifying the church; third, the reward of His sacrifice and labour of love wherein He will present the church to Himself in flawless perfection, "one pearl of great price." P. 1254.

Christ Living in the Believer. The Christian life is the outliving of the inliving Christ. "I am crucified with Christ; nevertheless I live; yet not I, but Christ liveth in me: and the life which I now live in the flesh I live by the faith of the Son of God, who loved me, and gave Himself for me." P. 1243.

Christ the Fulness of the Godhead. The "mystery of God" is Christ, as incarnating the fulness of the Godhead, and all the divine wisdom and knowledge for the redemption and reconciliation of man. P. 1263.

Godlikeness Restored to Man. Great is the mystery of godliness or of restoring the godlike qualities to man. So precious a result exalts all the plan and process in which "God was manifest in the flesh, justified in the Spirit, seen of angels, preached unto the Gentiles, believed on in the world, received up into glory" (1 Tim. 3. 16). P. 1276.

Working of Iniquity or Lawlessness. The working of the mystery of lawlessness under the divine restraint, which had already begun in Paul's time, shows the following phases: the apostasy of the professing church; the removal of that which restrains the mystery of lawlessness—no other than the Holy Spirit in the church, to be "taken out of the way;" the manifestation of the lawless one; the coming of Christ in glory and destruction of the lawless one (2 Thes. 2. 3-8). The outcome appears as the day of Jehovah. P. 1272.

The Seven Stars and Seven Candlesticks. In the seven churches and the messages to them there is given a foreview of the *spiritual* history of the church from say A. D. 96 to the end. Pp. 1331, 1332. See also Design B, Course VII, page 141 of these Courses.

"Babylon" Prefiguring Rome. The name Babylon, meaning "confusion," is repeatedly used by the prophets in a symbolic sense, and in its last mystic application in Scripture, in the book of Revelation, it denotes Rome ecclesiastically and politically. P. 1346.

Class Feature. Let the class consider how far it is the "mind of the Spirit" to lead true Christians to understand the mysteries of Scripture. P. 1138.

Questions

1. What is the ground for the use of the term mystery?
2. What aspects does Paul present bearing on the spiritual blindness of Israel?
3. To whom does the prospect of the translation of the saints apply?
4. What influence is greatest in making Christians of different races one body?
5. Can you give more than one way in which Christ's love-work for the church is shown?
6. What is the best proof that Christ lives in us?
7. Wherein is it revealed that Christ possesses the fulness of the Godhead?
8. Can we trace the process by which godliness is restored to man?
9. Do we know who is the "lawless one"? P. 1272.
10. Can you outline the course of spiritual history through the messages to the seven churches? Pp. 1331, 1332.

Program 6

KINGDOM PARABLES

Old Testament Prophets Limited. The Old Testament prophets saw in one blended vision the rejection and crucifixion of the King, and also His glory as David's Son, but "what manner of *time* the Spirit of Christ which was in them did signify when it testified beforehand the sufferings of Christ and the glory that should follow," was not revealed to them. That revelation Christ made in these parables of the kingdom.

Mysteries of the Kingdom of Heaven. A period of time is to intervene between Christ's sufferings and His glory, being occupied with the "mysteries of the kingdom of heaven," the considering of these coming over from the previous Program, because they are the subject of the seven kingdom parables found in the thirteenth chapter of Matthew. Taken together these parables describe the result of the presence of the Gospel in the world during the existing age, that is, the time of seed-sowing which began with our Lord's personal ministry and ends with the "harvest." Pp. 1014, 1015.

The Sower. This figure marks a new beginning. To labour in God's vineyard is one thing; to go forth sowing the seed of the word in a field which is the world is quite another. One-fourth of the seed takes permanent root, but the result is "wheat" or "children of the kingdom." This parable is treated throughout as foundational to the mysteries of the kingdom of heaven, and is interpreted by our Lord Himself. P. 1014.

The Tares Among the Wheat. This parable is also interpreted by Christ. Here the "good seed" is not the "word," as in the first parable, but rather that which the word has produced, namely: the children of the kingdom. These are providentially "sown," that is, scattered, here and there in the "field" of the "world." The "world" here is both geographical and ethnic—the earth-world, and also the world of men. The wheat of God at once becomes the scene of Satan's activity. Where children of the kingdom are gathered, there, "among the wheat," Satan "sows" "children of the wicked one," who profess to be children of the kingdom, and in outward ways are so like the true children that only the angels may, in the end, be trusted to separate them. So great is Satan's power of deception that the tares often really suppose themselves to be children of the kingdom (Matt. 7. 21–23). This parable is not a description of the world, but of that which professes to be the kingdom. Mere unbelievers are never called children of the devil, but only *religious* unbelievers. The gathering of the tares into bundles for burning does not imply immediate judgment. At the end of this age the tares are set aside for burning, but first the wheat is gathered into the barn. Pp. 1015, 1016.

The Grain of Mustard Seed. The parable of the mustard seed prefigures the rapid but unsubstantial growth of the mystery form of the kingdom from an insignificant beginning to a great place in the earth. The figure of the fowls finding shelter in the branches is drawn from Daniel 4. 20–22. How insecure was such a refuge the context in Daniel shows. P. 1016.

The Leaven. The interpretation of this parable which makes the leaven to be the Gospel, introduced into the world by the church, and working subtly until the world is converted is open to the objection that it does violence to the unvarying symbolical meaning of leaven, which in both the Old and New Testament is used in an evil sense. P. 1016.

The Hid Treasure. Our Lord is the buyer at the awful cost of His blood, and Israel, especially the lost tribes hidden in "the field," the world, is the treasure. The divine Merchantman buys the field (world) for the sake of the treasure. P. 1017.

The Pearl. As Israel is the hid treasure so the church is the pearl of great cost. Of the true church a pearl is a perfect symbol, formed by accretion, and that not mechanically, but vitally. P. 1017.

The Drag-net. The parable of the net presents another view from that of the wheat and tares. There Satan was the active agent; here the admixture is the result of the tendency of a movement to gather to itself that which is not really of it. P. 1018.

Class Feature. Let the leader canvass with the class this great subject of the mystery form of the Kingdom as given in essence in the foregoing paragraphs.

Questions

1. How was the vision of the Old Testament prophets limited as to the interval between Christ's sufferings and His glory? P. 1015.
2. Can you outline the time of the seed-sowing?
3. Are we now in this age?
4. What is the main point in the mystery teaching of the parable of the Sower?
5. Of the Tares among the Wheat?
6. Of the Grain of Mustard Seed?
7. Of the Leaven?
8. Of the Hid Treasure?
9. Of the Pearl?
10. Of the Drag-net?

Program 7

CRYPTIC BOOKS

The Problem of Job. It is the problem pervading the book of Job: "Why do the godly suffer?" rather than the qualities of the book itself that causes it to be placed among the cryptic, hidden, difficult, and challenging books of Scripture.

The Characters Sifted. The opening page of Course 3, which gives the line of approach, makes the sifting power of the cryptic books one of their distinguishing marks. Therefore it is not strange that these headings greet us: "In the sieve of Satan: mystery of God's permissive will"—"Again in Satan's sieve." Pp. 569, 570. Not alone Job, but other characters are sifted, such as the three "friends," and they prove to be dogmatists. Pp. 571, 574-576, while Elihu, though showing himself to be an eloquent orator, simply darkens counsel by words. P. 590.

Face to Face with Jehovah. Job at last is sifted by the just and loving words of Jehovah, and the answer to the problem is found: He has lost his self-righteous assurance and has won a true humility, when lo, he sees that *the godly are afflicted that they may gain self-knowledge and self-judgment that will lead to greater fruitfulness.* P. 597.

Class Feature. Let there be a brief offering from personal experience of members of the gains which comes from suffering. Compare lessons drawn from the present with those relating to Marah. "These bitter waters were in the very path of the Lord's leading, and stand for the trials of God's people, which are educatory and not punitive. The 'tree' is the cross (Gal. 3. 13) which became sweet to Christ as the expression of the Father's will (John 18. 11). When our Marahs are so taken we cast the 'tree' into the waters (Rom. 5. 3, 4)." P. 89.

Siftings of the Song of Solomon. It may be that the rule of the Jewish teachers was right, that young men should not read this book till they are thirty; and we may add young women not till they are twenty-five—that is, not read it with the confidence that they will see in it the pure ideals of love which in later years are made clear to many. No one can expect in adolescence the understanding that belongs to adult life. We are not to subject ourselves nor this book to unfair tests.

Back to First Things. We should note three things in connection with creation: First, when the work of creation—including man—was complete, God pronounced it "very good" (Gen. 1. 31); already, while the record states that "God created man in His own image," it also emphasizes the fact that "male and female created he them" (Gen. 1. 27); and then, as the creational sanction of marriage the method of the creation of woman is given, with this inference: "Therefore shall a man leave his father and mother and shall cleave unto his wife: and they shall be one flesh" (Gen. 2. 21-24). Turning now to the introduction to the Song of Solomon we read: "Primarily, the book is the expression of pure marital love as ordained of God in creation, and the vindication of that love as against both asceticism and lust—the two profanations of the holiness of marriage. The secondary and larger interpretation is of Christ the Son and His heavenly bride, the church." P. 705. This book, therefore, on the one hand, sifts all those who, instead of treating the elements of sex and marriage with reverence, turn them into matters of obscene imaginings, impure jokes, stories, and double meanings, and sensational and corrupting exploitation in plays and fiction; and, on the other hand, sifts many devout Christians who are too ascetic in their view of marriage. "The word 'Sister' (Song of Sol. 5. 1) here is of infinitely delicate significance, intimating the very whiteness of purity in the midst of an ardour which is, like the shekinah, aglow but unspeakably holy. Sin has almost deprived

us of the capacity even to stand with unshod feet before this burning bush."
P. 707.

Books of Daniel and Revelation. These books have long been counted among the most hidden as to meaning and difficult of full explanation, although the word *apokalupsis*, apocalypse or "unveiling," p. 1212, is a name for the closing prophetic book of the New Testament. That the two writings have many points of connection is pointed out. Daniel is the indispensable introduction to the New Testament prophecy, the themes of which are, the apostasy of the church, the manifestation of the man of sin, the great tribulation, the return of the Lord, the resurrections, and the judgments. These, except the first, are Daniel's themes also. P. 898. The interpretations of the many figures and symbolic series of these books are to be found at the places where they occur.

Questions

1. What questions give the problem of Job?
2. What happens to the other characters in the drama as well as to Job?
3. What term is applied to the three "friends" as a result of their sifting?
4. What finally changes the self-justifying spirit of Job?
5. What is the answer to the problem of the book?
6. Of what is the Song of Solomon primarily an expression? P. 705.
7. What is the secondary and larger interpretation? P. 705.
8. With what New Testament book is the book of Daniel closely connected?
9. What is the meaning of the word "Apocalypse"? P. 1212.
10. Can you give some of the themes shared by the books of Daniel and Revelation?

25 Review and Test Questions on Course III
(For directions see Note on page 29)

1. What is a type? P. 50.
2. What is a mystery, as understood in Scripture? P. 50.
3. How would you define a parable? Pp. 50, 51.
4. What are some of the veiled or cryptic books of the Bible? P. 51.
5. What typical meaning can we find in Eve? P. 52.
6. Of what kind of man is Cain a type? P. 52.
7. Of what quality or nature is Abel a type? P. 52.
8. In what way or ways can you speak of the tabernacle as a type? P. 54.
9. Can you give the typical meaning of the altar of incense and the incense offering? P. 54.
10. Of what is the showbread a type? P. 54.
11. In what points was Melchisedec a type of Christ? P. 56.
12. How does Aaron fill out the type of Christ as high priest? P. 56.
13. Of what later offerings were the bullock and the lamb in the sacrifices a type? P. 56.
14. Can you make a distinction between a type and a symbol? P. 58.
15. What is the world's most glorious symbol? P. 58.
16. In what Bible book does Christ appear under the symbols of the Lamb and the Lion? Pp. 58, 59.
17. Can you give a scripture verse or statement showing the mystery of Christ living in the believer? P. 60.
18. What is embodied in the mystery of Christ as the fulness of the Godhead? P. 60.
19. From about what year A. D. do the seven churches of the book of Revelation give a mystic foreview of the church-age? P. 61.
20. Can you give the names or general titles of some of the kingdom parables? P. 62.
21. In the parable of the leaven, is leaven to be taken in a good or in an evil sense? P. 62.
22. What may we consider is the meaning of the pearl of great price? P. 63.
23. What problem bearing on God's ways with man is seen in the book of Job? P. 64.
24. What is the conclusion as to why the godly are afflicted? P. 64.
25. Can you give the meaning of "Apocalypse," which is the real name of the book of Revelation? P. 65.

COURSE IV
CHRIST IN THE SCRIPTURES

COURSE IV

CHRIST IN THE SCRIPTURES

General View

1. Christ in the Pentateuch or "the Law."	4. Christ in the Gospels.
2. Christ in the Prophetical Books or "the Prophets."	5. Christ in the Book of Acts.
	6. Christ in the Epistles.
3. Christ in the Other Old Testament Books or "the Writings."	7. Christ in the Book of Revelation.

Progressive Bible Truth Concerning Christ. In the Panoramic View of the Bible, coming after the Introduction and the Preface, it is shown that the Bible is progressive in the unfolding of truth; and this applies to its unfolding of the truth concerning Christ. We read: "Nothing is told all at once, and once for all. Often with centuries between, one writer of Scripture takes up an earlier revelation, adds to it, lays down the pen, and in due time another man, moved by the Holy Spirit, and another, and another, add new details till the whole is complete." Again we read: "From beginning to end the Bible has one *great theme*—the person and work of the Christ."[1] These considerations furnish ample ground for extending Course IV throughout the entire Bible; and the progression is shown in the key words which mark the successive stages or phases of the Christ-theme.[1] The first of the five key-words is Preparation, and this covers the three Programs which correspond to the three Jewish divisions of the Old Testament, namely: The Law, the Prophets, and the Writings. The other four key-words—Manifestation, Propagation, Explanation, and Consummation—give the order of the four Programs which unfold the truth concerning Christ through the New Testament.

Gives Unity to the Bible. There was need, in the case of a book produced through so many centuries and by such an array of writers, of some element that would give unity to the whole. This should not be an idea, a doctrine, or a principle, valuable as these are, but a person, warm and winning, and such unquestionably our Lord has proved Himself to be. Christ, Son of God, Son of man, Son of Abraham, Son of David, thus binds the many books into one Book. Seed of the woman (Gen. 3. 15), He is the ultimate destroyer of Satan and his works; seed of Abraham, He is the world blesser; seed of David, He is Israel's King, yet also Desire of all Nations. Exalted to the right hand of God, He is "head over all to the church which is his body," while to Israel and the Nations the promise of His return forms the one and only rational expectation that humanity will yet fulfil itself.[2]

Christ at the Centre. Our Lord is exalted as the *central theme* of the Bible. The manifestation of Christ constitutes the Gospel, and to it all preceding Scripture leads, and from it all following Scripture proceeds.[2] Course IV is made to be central among these seven Bible Courses, and Design A[3] in the Foreword makes it the great equatorial belt uniting

---

[1] First page of the Panoramic View at front of Bible.
[2] Second page of Panoramic View.
[3] See page 8 of these Courses.

the Old and New Testament Hemispheres. For this Course Design A represents Christ as unrolling the scroll of Scripture and saying: "In the volume of the book it is written of me."

DESIGN A—CHRIST CENTRAL IN THE VOLUME OF SCRIPTURE

Program 1

CHRIST IN THE PENTATEUCH OR "THE LAW"

Redemption the Key-Idea. The Pentateuch, or five-fold writing, consisting of the five books with which the Old Testament opens, has a unity which has always been recognized, and by the Jews was called "the Law," being also called the books of Moses, or simply, for short, "Moses." An idea colours the whole body of truth in these books. God's people were chosen, and then by an alien nation were gradually enslaved and oppressed, and then by special divine power were delivered and led to the borders of their Promised Land. They, moreover, along with the rest of mankind, are shown as coming under the yoke of sin, through the tempting power of their adversary, and then are given a priesthood and careful gradation of offerings and sacrifices by which they can approach God and have their sin forgiven. Therefore, in the Pentateuch we see the people of Israel making concrete in their history and worship the truths of redemption and deliverance, of atonement and forgiveness which Christ by His sacrifice and Gospel of mercy has brought to the whole world. So it is not strange that we should find, as we have discovered in Programs 1–3 of Course III, that the typical foreshadowings of Christ form a literal network in the characters and ritual services of the Pentateuch. We will now examine other features which point to Christ in this section of the Bible.

Dawning Gospel Gleams. Hardly has the Pentateuch opened before we come to a statement which many Bible writers have honoured as the first gleam of a Gospel of Salvation. God is addressing the serpent through whose agency the fall of man has been brought about. He refers to the seed of the woman and says: "It shall bruise thy head and thou shalt bruise his heel" (Gen. 3. 15). Allusion has already been made to this early gleam of Gospel truth under the General View for this Course.[1] The next gleam is when God says to Abraham (Gen. 12. 3): "In thee shall all families of the earth be blessed." This is the great evangelic promise fulfilled in Abraham's Seed, Christ, and it brings into greater definiteness the promise of the Adamic Covenant concerning the Seed of the woman. P. 25.

Moses as a Type. Passing now to the book of Exodus, which is peculiarly the book of Redemption, p. 71, we see that Moses is a type of Christ the deliverer. First, He is a divinely chosen deliverer. Second, rejected by Israel He turns to the Gentiles. Third, during His rejection He gains a Gentile bride. Fourth, afterward He again appears as Israel's deliverer, and is accepted. Fifth, officially, Moses typifies Christ as Prophet, Advocate, Intercessor, and Leader, or King; while, in relation to the house of God, he is in contrast with Christ. Moses was faithful as a servant over another's house; Christ as a Son over His own house. P. 72.

The Passover Typical of Christ. The Passover was a type of Christ our Redeemer. First, the lamb must be without blemish, and to test this it was kept up four days. So our Lord's public life, under hostile scrutiny, was the testing which proved His holiness. Second, the lamb thus tested must be slain. Third, the blood must be applied. This answers to appropriation by personal faith, and refutes universalism. Fourth, the blood thus applied of itself, without anything in addition, constituted a perfect protection from judgment. P. 84.

Class Feature. Let the leader assign to one member the presenting of the items in which manna typifies Christ, p. 91; and to another the showing that the Nazarite type found its fulfilment in Jesus. Pp. 173, 174.

---

[1] See page 68 of these Courses.

Budding Rod and Christ's Resurrection. Aaron's rod that budded, was a type of Christ in resurrection, owned of God as High Priest. Aaron's priesthood had been questioned in the rebellion of Korah, so God Himself will confirm it. Each of the tribe-heads brought a perfectly dead rod; God put life into Aaron's only. So all the authors of religions have died, Christ among them, but only He was raised from the dead, and exalted to be a High Priest. P. 190.

Christ's Return and Israel's Future. The other books of the Pentateuch have contributed to this Program; and Deuteronomy, in giving the Palestinian Covenant, shows, among other points, the return of the Lord, restoration of Israel to the land, her national conversion, and judgment of her oppressors. P. 250. With these points we close our survey of Christ in the Pentateuch.

Questions

1. Of what books is the Pentateuch composed?
2. What were Jewish names for it?
3. What is its key-idea?
4. Where is found the first Gospel gleam in it?
5. What words give the second Gospel gleam or the "evangelic promise"?
6. In what ways is Moses a type of Christ?
7. How is the Passover typical of Christ?
8. What typical points are found in Manna? P. 91.
9. What truths are drawn from the budding of Aaron's rod?
10. What items of the Palestinian Covenant point to Christ? P. 250.

Program 2

CHRIST IN THE PROPHETICAL BOOKS OR "THE PROPHETS"

Yearning of the Prophets to Reveal Christ. Peter brings out the point that the prophets, scarcely knowing why they were so moved, nevertheless yearned to reveal our salvation as procured by Christ. (1 Pet. 1. 10–12.)

Messianic Character of Prophecy. When we grasp some of the great acts and covenants leading up to Christ's incarnation and mission, we perceive that the future blessing of Israel as a nation rests upon the Palestinian Covenant of restoration and conversion, p. 250, and the Davidic Covenant of the Kingship of the Messiah, David's Son, p. 362, and this gives predictive prophecy its Messianic character. The exaltation of Israel is secured in the Kingdom, and the Kingdom takes its power to bless from the Person of the King, David's Son, who is also "Immanuel," or God incarnate. P. 711.

Its Twofold Character. Having proceeded thus far we are confronted with these elements of the problem, that, as the King is also Son of Abraham and the promised Redeemer, and as redemption is only through the sacrifice of Christ, so Messianic prophecy of necessity presents Christ in a twofold character—a suffering Messiah such as we see in the fifty-third chapter of Isaiah, and a reigning Messiah, such as He is show 1 to be in the eleventh chapter of Isaiah. This duality, suffering and glory, weakness and power, involved a mystery which perplexed the prophets. P. 171.

Mystery Explained. The solution of this mystery lies, as the New Testament makes clear, in the two advents—the first advent to redemption through suffering; the second advent to the kingdom in glory, when the national promises to Israel will be fulfilled. The prophets indeed describe the advent in two forms which could not be contemporaneous, but to them it was not revealed that between the advent to suffering and the advent to glory would be accomplished certain "mysteries of the kingdom," nor that, consequent upon Messiah's rejection, the New Testament church would be called out. These were to them "mysteries hid in God." P. 711. See also Programs 5 and 6 of Course III, pp. 60-63 of these Courses.

Books of Daniel and Jonah. Gentile powers are mentioned as connected with Israel, but prophecy, save in Daniel, Obadiah, Jonah, and Nahum, is not *occupied* with Gentile world-history. P. 711. Two of these books—Daniel and Jonah—cause the personality of Christ to have an outlook toward the great Gentile portion of mankind.

Vision of Gentile World-Rule. Daniel is distinctively the prophet of "the times of the Gentiles." His vision sweeps the whole course of Gentile world-rule to its end in catastrophe, and to the setting up of the Messianic Kingdom. P. 898. Nebuchadnezzar's dream, as interpreted by Daniel, gives the course and end of "the times of the Gentiles," that is, of Gentile world-empire, and is fulfilled in Babylon, Media-Persia, Greece, and Rome. The latter power is seen divided first into two (the legs), fulfilled in the Eastern and Western Roman empires, and then into ten (the toes). Christ was put to death by the sentence of an officer of Rome, the fourth empire, which was then at the zenith of its power. Since the crucifixion the Roman empire has followed the course marked out in the vision, but Gentile world-dominion still continues. It is to end in a sudden catastrophic judgment (Armageddon), which is immediately followed by the Christ-rule of the Kingdom. He does not set up His kingdom till after the destruction of the Gentile world-system. P. 901.[1]

Class Feature. Let the leader and the class briefly discuss the historical outlook relating to the ten divisions of the former Roman Empire.

Questions

1. Where in the New Testament is it shown that the prophets yearned to reveal Christ?
2. On what Covenants did the future blessing of Israel rest? Pp. 250, 362, 711.
3. What character do these Covenants give predictive prophecy?
4. What must come to Christ as the promised Redeemer?
5. In what chapter of Isaiah is Christ especially shown as a suffering Messiah?
6. In what chapter as a reigning Messiah?
7. How are these opposite portrayals of Christ —one of suffering, the other of glory—harmonized?
8. What two prophetical books disclose that Christ has an outlook toward the Gentile world?
9. Whose vision did Daniel interpret which revealed Christ's final effect on Gentile world-rule?
10. Can you give the series of materials making up the image, and for what each stands, and then the form in which Christ enters, and then the result?

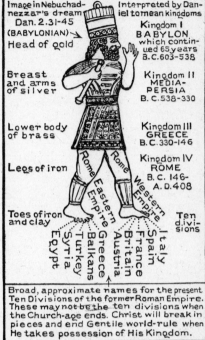

Image in Nebuchadnezzar's dream Dan. 2.31-45 (BABYLONIAN) Head of gold

Breast and arms of silver

Lower body of brass

Legs of iron

Toes of iron and clay

Interpreted by Daniel to mean kingdoms

Kingdom I BABYLON which continued 65 years B.C.603-538

Kingdom II MEDIA-PERSIA B.C.538-330

Kingdom III GREECE B.C.330-146

Kingdom IV ROME B.C. 146-A.D.408

Ten divisions

Rome Eastern Empire Greece Balkans Turkey Syria Egypt

Rome Western Empire Austria Britain France Spain Italy

Broad, approximate names for the present Ten Divisions of the former Roman Empire. These may not be the ten divisions when the Church-age ends. Christ will break in pieces and end Gentile world-rule when He takes possession of His Kingdom.

DESIGN B—GENTILE WORLD-RULE AND CHRIST'S KINGDOM

[1] See also Program 8 and Design B of Course VII, pages 140-142 of these Courses.

Program 3

CHRIST IN THE PSALMS

Covering the Old Testament. The Hebrew Bible, or our Old Testament, has three divisions. Christ has been viewed in the Law and the Prophets. There is left the third division, called by the Jews "Writings," made up of thirteen books. Among these the Psalms stand first, so they may represent the Writings, and to this extent Christ is traced in all the Old Testament Scriptures.

Path of Approach. The simplest description of the five books of Psalms is that they were the inspired prayer-and-praise book of Israel. The Psalms in which Christ is most fully portrayed are called Messianic Psalms. P. 599. In Design C we may think of the five books of Psalms as if they were zones or sections in a railway map. Then we follow the indicated route from left to right, and the named stations are the Messianic Psalms. Where Christ is shown in trial and humiliation, the route descends; where He is exalted, it rises up.

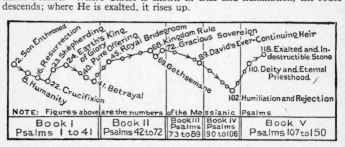

DESIGN C—MESSIANIC PROGRESS AND STATIONS OF CHRIST IN THE PSALMS

Son Enthroned. In the second Psalm, opening the Messianic line, we see Christ the Son at first rejected, enthroned as King upon Zion. P. 600.

Humanity. In the eighth Psalm, while Christ's deity is fully recognized, He is seen as Son of man. P. 602.

Resurrection. The sixteenth Psalm predicts Christ's resurrection. At some time subsequent to this event He assumes the Davidic throne. P. 605.

Crucifixion. The twenty-second Psalm is a graphic picture of death by crucifixion. There is given a series of physical details which are all incidental to that mode of death; and the accompanying circumstances, such as the period of darkness and the casting of lots for the clothes, were literally fulfilled. P. 608.

Shepherding by Earth's King of Glory. At this point there is a triple station or trilogy. In the twenty-second Psalm the *good* Shepherd gives His life for the sheep; in the twenty-third the *great* Shepherd tenderly cares for the sheep; in the twenty-fourth the *chief* Shepherd appears as King of glory to own and reward the sheep. P. 608.

Pure Offering. The fortieth Psalm contains the declarations in verses six to eight which are attributed to Christ in the tenth chapter of Hebrews. When sacrifice and offering had become abominable because of the wickedness of the people, the obedient Servant came to make the pure offering. P. 618.

74

Betrayal. The forty-first Psalm is the Psalm of the betrayal of the Son of man, as Jesus Himself taught. (John 13. 18, 19). P. 618.

Royal Bridegroom. The forty-fifth Psalm obviously looks forward to the advent of Christ in kingly glory. When the church is presented as the queen, the King is called *Adonai* (Lord, verse eleven), the husband name of Deity. P. 620.

Kingdom Rule. In the sixty-eighth Psalm occur events connected with Christ's ascension ministry and kingdom rule, and we recognize the pervasive joy of Israel in the kingdom. P. 630.

Gethsemane. In the sixty-ninth Psalm, verses fourteen to twenty may well describe the exercises of Christ's holy soul in Gethsemane. P. 631.

Gracious Sovereign. The seventy-second Psalm forms a complete vision of Messiah's kingdom so far as the Old Testament revelation extended. The emphatic word is righteousness, and universal blessing is to be brought in. Pp. 633, 634.

David's Ever-Continuing Heir. The eighty-ninth Psalm confirms and explains the Davidic Covenant. The covenant looks far beyond David and Solomon, even to Immanuel. P. 643.

Humiliation and Rejection. Since the first chapter of Hebrews makes reference to verses twenty-five to twenty-seven of the hundred and second Psalm, we are assured that in the preceding verses of the Psalm we are shown Christ in the days of His humiliation and rejection. P. 648.

Deity and Eternal Priesthood. The hundred and tenth Psalm affirms the deity of Jesus, and announces His eternal priesthood. Pp. 654, 655.

Exalted and Indestructible Stone. The Messianic progress of Christ in the Psalms closes at this high station, when, in the hundred and eighteenth Psalm He is shown in His final exaltation as the indestructible "head stone of the corner" (verse 22). P. 657.

Class Feature. Let the leader briefly review the Messianic teaching in the Old Testament.

Questions

1. What are the three divisions of the Hebrew Bible?
2. Where do the Psalms stand among the Writings?
3. What are the Psalms?
4. Into how many books are they divided?
5. What are the Psalms revealing Christ called?
6. How many are surveyed in this Program?
7. Which Psalms is named "Son Enthroned"?
8. Which one "Crucifixion"?
9. Which one "Royal Bridegroom"?
10. Which one "Gracious Sovereign"?

Program 4

CHRIST IN THE GOSPELS

Manifestation. The first page of the Panoramic View, at the front of the Bible we are studying, makes a fivefold division of the Bible, with Christ as the controlling figure from the first to the last of the Scriptures. The Old Testament, through which the first three Programs of this Course have taken us, is the *Preparation* for Christ; the Gospels give His *Manifestation.*

Relation of the Old Testament to the New. The Old Testament is a divinely provided Introduction to the New; and whoever comes to the study of the four Gospels with a mind saturated with the Old Testament foreview of Christ, His person, work, and kingdom, will make the right approach to understanding Christ incarnate. P. 989.

What the Gospels Record. The four Gospels record the eternal being, human ancestry, birth, death, resurrection, and ascension of Jesus the Christ, Son of God and Son of Man. They record also a selection from the incidents of His life and from His words and works. Taken together, they set forth, not a biography but a Personality. P. 989.

The Important Thing. That which is important is that through these narratives we should come to see and know Him whom they reveal. It did not please God to cause to be written a biography of His Son. But the four Gospels, though designedly incomplete as a story, are divinely perfect as a revelation. We may not through them know everything that He did, but we may know the Doer. In four great characters, each of which completes the other three, we have Jesus Christ Himself set forth —by what He said and did. P. 989.

Class Feature. Let there be brief prayer by the leader and others for true spiritual knowledge of the written oracles and of the living Christ. Design D may be considered as embodying in one view the essence of the fourfold Gospel revelation, touching the derivation, genealogy, birth, character, function, purpose, distinction, and contrasting elements of the Christ Personality.

PERSONALITY OF CHRIST			
POINTS OF COMPARISON	**MATTHEW**	**MARK**	**LUKE**	**JOHN**
Derivation	Davidic Covenant Abrahamic Covenant		Adamic Covenant	Pre-existence
Genealogy	Genealogy of Joseph		Genealogy of Mary	Only Begotten Son
Birth	Infant Adored by Magi		Manger Babe and Inquiring Boy	Incarnation
Character	Messiah	Master	Elder Brother	The Word (Logos)
Function	Prophet-Teacher	Wonder-Worker	Seeker of the Lost	The Way, the Truth, the Life
Purpose	Establishing the Kingdom of Heaven	Mighty One to Heal and Redeem	Bringing in the Kingdom of God	Manifesting Love Divine
Distinction	Son of God	Saviour	Son of Man	The Light of the World
Contrasting Elements	King	Servant	Man	God

DESIGN D—UNITED VIEW OF CHRIST IN THE FOUR GOSPELS

Themes and Names in Matthew. Matthew writes of Jesus called Christ as covenanted King. Christ, the Greek form of the Hebrew "Messiah," is the official name of our Lord, as Jesus is His human name. The name, "Christ," connects Him with the entire Old Testament foreview of a coming Prophet, Priest, and King. As these were typically anointed

76

with oil, so Jesus was anointed with the Holy Spirit, thus becoming officially "the Christ."   P. 994.

Theme of Mark. In Mark Jesus is seen as the mighty Worker, rather than as the unique Teacher.   P. 1045.

Theme of Luke. Luke is the Gospel of the human-divine One, and its key-phrase is "Son of man."   P. 1070.

Theme of John. The theme of this Gospel is the incarnation of the eternal Word, to reveal God in the terms of human life.   P. 1114.

Questions

1. What word embodies the service of the four Gospels respecting Christ?
2. What can the Old Testament be called in relation to the New?
3. What do the Gospels set forth about Christ?
4. What supremely important thing are the Gospels designed to do for us?
5. What is the theme of Matthew?
6. Of our Lord's two names which is personal and which official?
7. What is their meaning?
8. What is the theme of Mark?
9. What is the theme of Luke?
10. What is the theme of John?

Program 5

CHRIST IN THE BOOK OF ACTS

Propagation. The term in the Panoramic View expressive of the service of the book of Acts respecting Christ is *Propagation.* However, we may note that not so directly does the written record in this case serve as it does in the case of the Gospels. They directly and continuously through the church-age manifest Christ. The book of Acts historically records and preserves for its example and stimulus the work of Christ-propagation carried forward by the apostolic church; but each generation of Christians must accomplish its own work of calling out, or propagation ceases.

The Holy Spirit Magnifies Christ. The Holy Spirit fills the scene in this record of opening church life, but only to magnify Christ. As the presence of the Son, exalting and revealing the Father, is the great fact of the Gospels, so the presence of the Spirit, exalting and revealing the Son, is the great fact of the Acts. P. 1147.

Resurrection-Ministry of Christ. As the book opens there is a little space during which, before His ascension, Christ *personally* ministered. For forty days the risen Lord instructed the apostles "of the things pertaining to the kingdom of God," doubtless, according to His custom, teaching them out of the Scriptures. One point was left untouched, namely, the time when He would restore the kingdom to Israel; hence the apostles' question. The answer was according to His repeated teaching; the *time* is God's secret. But in a real sense Christ, though ascended to the Father, still carries forward His ministry on earth. In the Acts of the Apostles Luke extends the account of Christianity begun in the Gospel which bears His name. In the "former treatise" he tells what Jesus "began both to do and teach"; in the Acts what Jesus continued to do and teach through His Holy Spirit sent down. P. 1147.

Why Peter Came to the Front. As respects the human element the first chapter of Acts discloses the apostle Peter in the place of leadership of the little group of Christians. His personal qualities would naturally lead him to take such a place. Moreover, gratitude for his restored apostleship would impel him to step into this position of danger. Still further, Christ had committed to him the keys, or the right to open the kingdom, by discipleship, to Jews and Gentiles.

Christ is Preached. Following the direction of Christ the company of disciples continued in prayer in the upper room until the Holy Spirit was poured out on the day of Pentecost. Then Peter stood up and preached Christ to the great throng of Jews gathered from all countries as well as to the rulers, showing that Jesus is the Messiah. No message could have been more unwelcome to the Jews who had rejected Christ's Messianic claims and crucified Him. P. 1150. In Peter's second sermon the appeal was to the Jewish people as such, and not to individuals as in his first sermon. In that sermon those who were pricked in heart were exhorted to save themselves from (among) the untoward nation; but in the next sermon the whole people is addressed, and the promise to *national* repentance is *national* deliverance: Peter saying: "and he (God) shall send Jesus Christ" to bring in the times which the prophets had foretold. The official answer was the imprisonment of the apostles and the inhibition to preach. P. 1153.

Jews Reject Messiah. In the persecutions of the apostles and finally in the martyrdom of Stephen, the Jews sent after their King, Jesus, the message of rejection: "We will not have this man to reign over us." P. 1147. But this did not stop the work of propagation. Saul, soon to become Paul, was the arch-persecutor, and after Stephen "fell asleep," fierce persecution caused the church at Jerusalem to be scattered abroad, and they "went everywhere preaching the word." P. 1159.

Christ Everywhere on the Field. The entire movement and atmosphere of Acts creates the conviction that Christ is the living leader, present everywhere on the field. It is His power that heals the lame man at the gate of the temple; His presence with the workers that makes them fearless. The martyred Stephen sees Him standing in an attitude of heavenly interest; and at the vision of His glory Saul the persecutor falls powerless to the earth and pledges allegiance. Thenceforward to the very end of Acts this new Master appears to be directing the chief apostle's restless energies and to be working out his victories.

Class Feature. The leader in conference with the class should consider Christ's present call to propagation.

Questions

1. What is the key-idea for the book of Acts?
2. Is this idea attached to the record or to the Christian life and action that lay back of the record?
3. What does the Holy Spirit especially do with respect to Christ in the book of Acts?
4. What instruction did Christ give the apostles during the forty days?
5. Why did Christ not tell them when He would restore the kingdom to Israel?
6. What apostle became the first leader of the church?
7. In connection with what occurrence did Peter give his first sermon?
8. What events made it clear that the Jewish people still rejected Jesus as Messiah?
9. At what junctures did Christ's appearances insure His leadership?
10. At what points of need did He give strength to Paul?

Program 6

CHRIST IN THE EPISTLES

Explanation. The word respecting Christ which embraces and distinguishes the Epistles is *explanation.* It is a strong and truly expressive word, and such it needs to be, for it stands for the service of twenty-one books out of twenty-seven in the New Testament, and covers the output of probably six different writers. Some of these books are brief, but they are intensive, and coming, as they do, near the close of the whole volume of inspired Scripture, they seem surcharged with spiritual thought and weighty with revealed truth.

Christ Central and Supreme. As soon as we begin to survey this field we find that Christ is the central and commanding figure throughout the Epistles. If at times the church appears as the overshadowing theme, it is intended that we should see that "the church is not an organization, but an organism, the body of Christ, instinct with His life, and heavenly in calling, promise, and destiny." P. 1189. Paul is the writer of thirteen (not counting Hebrews) out of the twenty-one Epistles; and he, "converted by the personal ministry of the Lord in glory, is distinctively the witness to a glorified Christ, Head over all things to the church which is His body, as the Eleven were to Christ in the flesh." P. 1189. Therefore, in the leading Epistles of Paul, the great epistolary writer, in this twofold way, first, directly in His own person, and second, as Head of the church, Christ Jesus our Lord is supreme.

Exalting Language. Throughout his Epistles Paul uses many expressions which exalt Christ. If salvation is the great inclusive word of the Gospel, what is its highest-reaching ideal for the believer? Certainly it calls for righteousness and conformity to Christ. P. 1192. Justification and righteousness are inseparably united in Scripture. Christ has made propitiation by His sacrifice, and He becomes our righteousness when we receive Him by faith, and God justifies us. P. 1195. In Christ, the good olive tree, we attain a corporate life. P. 1204. In Him, our risen and glorified Head, we are organically united with each other. P. 1222.

Christ's Place in Other Epistles. James, termed "the Lord's brother," appears not to have accepted Jesus as the Messiah till after His resurrection. Then he became a disciple and the leader of the Jerusalem church. His Epistle, probably written earliest of all, opens with the words: "James, a servant of God and of the Lord Jesus Christ," p. 1306, making the Master co-equal with God in honour. The words of one writer concerning him are "We feel that he has his eye ever on his Holy Brother as he writes." The author of the Epistle to the Hebrews, whom students have not agreed on, makes Christ the antitype fulfilling all the typical significance of the tabernacle, priesthood, and sacrificial aim of the Old Testament system. P. 1291. The Epistles of Peter, Jude, and John especially lay stress on holding to the faith, and the great object of this faith is Christ's incarnation, reality, and continuing life. Pp. 1311–1313, 1317, 1320, 1321, 1326, 1328. See also Design E.

Class Feature. Let the leader and class develop a written list of terms and expressions in the Epistles which show the commanding rank and service of Christ.

Questions

1. What is the term which includes and interprets all the Epistles?
2. How many probable writers of the Epistles were there?
3. Why do the Epistles appear to be closely packed with truth?

4. What is the position of Christ in the Epistles?
5. When the truth concerning the church is emphasized, why do the Epistles still exalt Christ?
6. What phrase in the Epistles may be chosen as giving Christ the greatest place? .
7. What is the attitude of James toward Chirst in this field?
8. Of Peter?
9. Of Jude?
10. Of John?

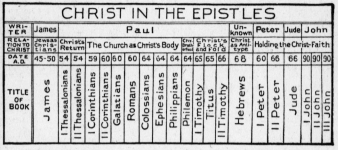

CHRIST IN THE EPISTLES																					
WRITER	James	Paul														Unknown	Peter		Jude	John	
RELATION TO CHRIST	Jewsas Christians	Christ's Return	The Church as Christ's Body								Chr. Brotherhood	Christ's Flock and Fold			Christ as Antitype	Holding the Christ-Faith					
DATE A.D.	45-50	54	54	59	60	60	60	64	64	64	64	65	65	66	68	60	66	66	90	90	90
TITLE OF BOOK	James	I Thessalonians	II Thessalonians	I Corinthians	II Corimthians	Galatians	Romans	Colossians	Ephesians	Philippians	Philemon	I Timothy	Titus	II Timothy	Hebrews	I Peter	II Peter	Jude	I John	II John	III John

DESIGN E—WRITER, RELATION TO CHRIST, AND DATE OF EPISTLES

Program 7

CHRIST IN THE BOOK OF REVELATION

Consummation. In this book of Revelation all the purposes of God in and through Christ are consummated.[1] It is at one and the same time the consummation of the manifestation and mission of Christ as respects the earth, and the consummation of the process of divine redemption culminating in the end-things. While Christ is the central theme of the book, all of the events move toward one consummation, the bringing in of the covenanted kingdom. The key-phrase is the prophetic declaration of Rev. 11. 15; (literally) "The world kingdom of our Lord and of his Christ has come." The book is therefore a prophecy (1. 3). P. 1330. The unfolding of the broad outline and steps of this prophecy is shown in Design F.

Christ's Present Position. When our Lord says (Rev. 3. 21): "I am set down with my Father in his throne," it is conclusive that He is not now seated upon His own throne. The Davidic covenant, and the promises of God through the prophets and the angel Gabriel concerning the Messianic kingdom await fulfilment. P. 1334.

The Antichrist. Antichrist the *person* is to be distinguished from the "many antichrists" and the "spirit of antichrist" which characterizes all. The supreme mark of all is the denial of the Christian truth of the incarnation of the *Logos* the eternal Son in Jesus as the Christ. The many "antichrists" precede and prepare the way for *the* Antichrist, who is "the Beast out of the earth," and the "false prophet." He is the last ecclesiastical head, as the Beast of Rev. 13. 4-8 is the last civil head. For the purposes of persecution he is permitted to exercise the autocratic power of the emperor-Beast. Pp. 1342, 1343.

The All-conquering Christ. While Christ in the book of Revelation is not yet seated upon His own throne, He is prophetically made all-conquering, as He will be when the Kingdom is consummated. Looking backward and forward passages sum up results accomplished, and speak of results yet to come as if they had already come. P. 1330. In essence His rule is shown by the Old Testament prophets to secure such conditions as these: the meek, not the proud, will inherit the earth; longevity will be greatly increased; the knowledge of the Lord will be universal; beast ferocity will be removed; absolute equity will be enforced; and the enormous majority of earth's inhabitants will be saved. P. 977. Design F indicates the path to such an age of victory.

Class Feature. Let there be a conference and then prayer for the power to see the all-conquering Christ more fully in the Scriptures and in life.

Questions

1. In what sense is Revelation the consummation of Christ's mission?
2. In what of God's purpose in world history?
3. In what of the divine aim in redemption?
4. What is the present position of Christ as respects His throne?
5. What is the supreme mark of the Antichrist element?
6. Into what does it head up in the end?
7. How do you distinguish the Beast and the False Prophet?
8. Can you describe some scenes of Revelation that show the victorious Christ?
9. What are the three divisions of Revelation? P. 1330 and Design F.
10. Can you give the seven sevens of Revelation by a word or short title? P. 1330 and Design F.

[1] See Panoramic View at front of Bible.

CHRIST IN THE BOOK OF REVELATION

DIVISION II—The Church Age "Write...the things which are." Rev. 2:1-3:22		DIVISION III— "Write...the things	The things
1st "Seven" of Revelation, composed of the seven churches of chapters 2 and 3 which form the foreview of the Church-age. See pages 1330-1332 and Design B, (Course VII) 1. Ephesus 2. Smyrna 3. Pergamos 4. Thyatira 5. Sardis 6. Philadelphia 7. Laodicea	2d "Seven" SEALS Rev. 4:1-8:1 1. Pestilence 2. War 3. Famine 4. Death 5. Martyred remnant 6. Anarchy 7. Yields 7 Trumpets	3d "Seven" TRUMPETS Rev. 8:2-11:19 With relation to 1. Trees and grass 2. Sea life and ships 3. Water of rivers 4. Sources of light 5. Terrible locusts 6. Destroying host 7. Judgment and reward	
4th "Seven" PERSONAGES Rev. 12:1-14:20 1. The Woman: Israel 2. Satan 3. The Child: Christ 4. The archangel 5. The Jewish remnant 6. Beast out of the sea 7. Beast out of the earth	5th "Seven" BOWLS Rev. 15:1-16:21 causing 1. Grievous sore 2. Sea of blood 3. Bloody rivers 4. Scorching sun 5. Darkness and pain 6. Dried up Euphrates 7. Earthquake and hail	6th "Seven" DOOMS Rev. 17:1-20:15 1. Babylon: Rome 2. The Beast 3. The False Prophet 4. Kings 5. Gog and Magog 6. Satan 7. Unbelieving dead	7th "Seven" NEW THINGS Rev. 21:1-22:21 1. New heaven 2. New earth 3. New peoples 4. New Jerusalem 5. New temple 6. New light 7. New Paradise

Kingdom Age which shall be hereafter." Rev. 4:1-22:21

REVELATION

DIVISION I—The Patmos Vision "Write the things which thou hast seen."—Rev. 1:9-18

Christ is seen in the midst of the seven candlesticks or churches, and kindling them from His right hand, while ready to maintain and defend them by the two edged sword, "the Word of God," which has proceeded from His mouth.

DESIGN F—THE THREE DIVISIONS AND SEVEN "SEVENS" OF REVELATION

25 Review and Test Questions on Course IV
(For directions see Note on page 29)

1. What shows that the Bible is progressive in the unfolding of truth? P. 68.

2. When "Preparation" is used as a key-idea for the Old Testament, it means preparation for what or whom? P. 68.

3. How is unity given to the various parts of the Scriptures? P. 68.

4. How would you show that Christ is central in the Bible? P. 68.

5. Can you give some ways in which Moses, the chief character of the Pentateuch, is typical of Christ? P. 70.

6. What points about the passover make it typical of Christ? P. 70.

7. How does the budding of Aaron's rod designate Christ as the one living leader? P. 71.

8. What is meant by the Messianic character of prophecy? P. 72.

9. Can you cite or suggest passages in the prophetic writings which make Christ or a coming one kingly, wise, exalted, powerful? P. 72.

10. Is he represented as overturning future kingdoms? P. 72.

11. What are the Psalms called which use language most closely applicable to Christ? P. 74.

12. In which Psalm is Christ as the Son seated upon the holy hill of Zion? P. 74.

13. What Psalm makes our divine Lord a Shepherd? P. 74.

14. Can you give the key-word for the disclosure of Christ in the Gospels? P. 76.

15. Do the Gospels aim to set forth Christ's biography or his personality? P. 76.

16. Can you give, in a word or sentence, the view of Christ in each Gospel? Pp. 76, 77.

17. What is the one word for the church making Christ known in Acts? P. 78.

18. What new Agent from above is at work in Acts? P. 78.

19. Yet who from above is still more the Leader on the field? P. 79.

20. What is the key-word for the Epistles, in further making Christ known? P. 80.

21. What is the main theme of Paul's Epistles? P. 80.

22. How does James, termed "the Lord's brother," honour Christ in his Epistle? P. 80.

23. What is the final key-word used for the Christ-message of the last Bible book? P. 82.

24. Can you give briefly your idea of the Antichrist? P. 82.

25. How does Christ overmatch the adversary? P. 82.

COURSE V

PROPHECY

General View

PROPHETS—PERIOD AND FIELD. P. 712.

A. Before the Exile.
  1. Elijah and Elisha: Prophets to Israel (Non-writing).
  2. Obadiah and Joel: Prophets to Judah.
  3. Amos and Hosea: Prophets to Israel.
  4. Jonah: Prophet to Nineveh.
  5. Isaiah and Micah: Prophets to Judah.
  6. Nahum, Zephaniah, Habakkuk, and Jeremiah: Prophets to Judah.
B. During the Exile.
  7. Ezekiel and Daniel: Prophets to Judah.
C. After the Exile.
  8. Haggai, Zechariah, and Malachi: Prophets to Judah.

Type of Men. Prophets were men raised up of God in times of declension and apostasy among His ancient people. They were primarily revivalists and patriots, speaking on behalf of God to the heart and conscience of the nation. It is necessary to keep this Israelitish character of the prophet in mind. He is not a detached and abstract thinker, but has in view the covenant people, their sin and failure, their awakening and restoration to faithfulness, and their glorious future. P. 711.

Messianic Feature. Foremost among key points in the field of prophecy stands the ideal of the Messiah, already considered in Program 5, Course III, on "Leading Mysteries"[1] and more fully unfolded in Program 2, Course IV, on "Christ in the Prophetical Books."[2]

Hebrew Pattern. The conception of the Hebrew people, as called of God and chosen for a high spiritual mission, forms a prophetic pattern that enters into all prophecy. As the Christian ministry of any given country or nation of our time has an ideal for the life and future history of that nation, so did the Hebrew prophets have for their nation. One part of that ideal was the person and work of the Messiah just referred to. Another chief section of the prophetic pattern for Israel was the outlook on Hebrew destiny furnished by the Palestinian Covenant, p. 250, which has been considered in Program 4 of Course II.[3] Its main features were woven by the fact of Israel's defection and departure from God, running through so much of her history; the persistent and unescapable travail of the infinite, divine Lover seeking to win His chosen to return to Him; and the means that could best reconstitute right relations. At this juncture the Gentile peoples come into view, since God can use them for the chastening of Israel. They in their turn will be judged for blind and selfish severities, and ways will be found by which they can also share in the grace that must finally reclaim God's own. The doctrine of the Remnant —a saving faithful few who preserve the true Israelitish life in times of

---

[1] Page 60 of these Courses. [2] Page 72 of these Courses.
[3] Page 41 of these Courses.

86

extreme declension—is a marked feature of the pattern, as is also the vision of the Kingdom, that is to guard the framework of the theocracy and the tribes, lost though they may seem to be for centuries, to arise in triumph and splendour at the end. That end will also unroll a great climacteric period belonging in the prophetic pattern—the Day of the Lord. Pp. 711, 712. See also Program 8 and Design B, Course VII.[1]

Near and Far View. The prophetic messages have a twofold character: first, that which is local and for the prophet's time; second, that which is predictive of the divine purpose in the future. P. 711. Design A shows that the main prophetic era covered five centuries, from B. C. 900 to 400. Furthermore, the prophetic spirit may be said to reach backward and to touch such characters as Jacob, Moses, Samuel, and David; and forward to embrace John the Baptist, Christ our Lord, and St. John.

DESIGN A—PERIODS OF PROPHETS WITH LISTS OF KINGS

Program 1

ELIJAH AND ELISHA

Duality and Service. In several of the Programs of this Course we shall find two personalities associated in service, or at least ministering as prophets in the same field as respects Northern or Southern Kingdom at somewhere near the same time. There appears to be a suggestion of a law of duality among leaders who extend the spiritual kingdom. Moses closely wrought with Aaron or later with Joshua. The Master sent the seventy out two by two. Peter and John, Paul and Barnabas, are other examples. The two thus associated often present a contrast in disposition. If one might prove too sanguine and bold, the more quiet nature of his associate acts as a balance. In view of the mutual interaction of such relations we feel that Elisha is aptly paired with Elijah.

Action before Writing. These two non-writing prophets come upon the scene a little before the succession begins of those who commit their prophecies to writing. Here again we seem to meet with the working of an inner law of our life. First the deed breaking through the set order of things like lava from a volcano; then the word which records this startling movement and tries to interpret it. Years went by after Christ accomplished His wondrous earthly mission before the agitated mind of man became reposeful enough to engrave the story of what had happened in Gospel and Epistle and Apocalypse. The first step in that era of action was taken when John the Baptist appeared in the wilderness of Judea; and another man of this same type begins the long period of Old Testament prophecy when Elijah, unheralded by any statement of his birth or lineage, suddenly appears before King Ahab, saying: "As the Lord God liveth, before whom I stand, there shall not be dew nor rain these years, but according to my word." Thus does the ministry of Elijah begin with his prediction of a three years' drought. P. 411.

Call for Rocklike Strength. If prophets are called to be revivalists, as it has been stated, clearly the Northern Kingdom, made up of Ten Tribes that had revolted under Jeroboam, demanded a man of the type of Elijah at this time. Only a personality of rocklike strength could believe a revival of true faith possible over against the baseness of King Ahab, the sinister influence of Jezebel the queen, and the national drift toward Baal worship.

Class Feature. Let the leader consider with the class the power of lives hidden in the secret of the divine presence.

Tracing the Prophet. In Design B, section *1* shows Elijah's course in coming from Gilead east of the Jordan to meet King Ahab at or near Samaria, his capital. The three years' drought is announced and Elijah goes *2.* to the brook Cherith. Then there follow: *3.* to Zarephath, *4.* back to Samaria at the end of three years and the second meeting of Ahab, thence *5.* to Mt. Carmel, *6.* back to Jezreel, *7.* the long journey to Horeb or Mt. Sinai, with the scenes of Elijah's despair near Beer-sheba and of God's disclosure at Sinai, then *8.* the return journey to Jezreel.

Elisha. To Elisha was committed a more quiet work. He conserved the results of the better agencies that were put in motion by Elijah.

Questions

1. In which of the two kingdoms did Elijah and Elisha do their prophetic work?
2. Can you cite an instance in the life of Christ when He arranged workers two by two?

3. What two apostles served together and where?
4. What is the advantage of this dual plan?
5. What New Testament herald resembles Elijah?
6. Who were the king and queen when Elijah appeared?
7. Where did Elijah take refuge during the famine?
8. What place beheld his great triumph.
9. To what distant place did he go when discouraged?
10. What term applies to Elisha's work?

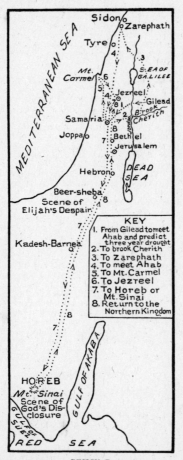

KEY

1. From Gilead to meet Ahab and predict three year drought
2. To brook Cherith
3. To Zarephath
4. To meet Ahab
5. To Mt. Carmel
6. To Jezreel
7. To Horeb or Mt. Sinai
8. Return to the Northern Kingdom

DESIGN B

MAIN MOVEMENTS OF ELIJAH

89

Program 2

OBADIAH AND JOEL

Period of Obadiah and Joel. While some writers would place Obadiah about two hundred years later than Elijah and Elisha, bringing him into the general period of Jeremiah, there are others who give him the earlier date. "Internal evidence seems to fix the date of Obadiah's ministry in the reign of the bloody Athaliah (2 Ki. 8. 16–26). If this be true, and if the ministry of Joel was during the reign of Joash, then Obadiah is chronologically first of the writing prophets." P. 941. Joel also comes in this general period. "Joel, a prophet of Judah, probably exercised his ministry during the reign of Joash (2 Chron. 22–24). In his youth he may have known Elijah, and he certainly was a contemporary of Elisha." P. 930.

Declension and Divine Help. When the spirit of good and of God's service was weakened in the Northern Kingdom, and it seemed as if Baal, the god of the Sidonians, to the northwest of Israel, was to triumph among the Israelitish people, largely through the influence of Jezebel, a Sidonian who had become the wife of King Ahab (2 Ki. 16. 31), God turned the heart of the northern tribes back to Himself through the work of Elijah and Elisha. But the wave of declension also swept over the Southern Kingdom. Athaliah, daughter of Ahab and Jezebel, became queen mother there, and usurped and held authority for six years; and God raised up for Judah's help two prophets, Obadiah and Joel. Thus this quartette of inspired men fulfil the main idea of prophecy; they are revivalists and restorers of the true faith in a time of need. Baal worship was exterminated in Israel (2 Ki. 10. 19–28): and when Athaliah was slain its beginnings in Judah were also destroyed (2 Ki. 11. 17–19).

Class Feature. Let the class consider the doctrine of the Remnant in the pattern of prophecy, starting with God's assurance to Elijah at Horeb: "Yet I have left me seven thousand in Israel, all the knees which have not bowed unto Baal, and every mouth which hath not kissed him" (1 Ki. 19. 18). In Isaiah's time it was the "very small remnant" for whose sake God still forebore to destroy the nation. During the captivities the remnant appears in Jews like Ezekiel and Daniel, the three delivered from the fiery furnace, and Esther and Mordecai. At the end of the seventy years of Babylonian captivity it was the remnant which returned under Zerubbabel and Ezra. At the advent of our Lord, John the Baptist, Simeon, Anna, and others looking "for redemption" were the remnant. During the Church-age the remnant is composed of believing Jews. In the great tribulation preceding Christ's second advent a remnant out of all Israel will turn to him as Messiah, and will become His witnesses after the removal of the church. Some of these will undergo martyrdom, and some will be spared to enter the millennial kingdom. P. 1205.

Obadiah and Edom. The short written prophecy of Obadiah, so brief that it is not divided into chapters, is almost wholly taken up with Edom. The Edomites, as descended from Esau, might be called the cousins of Judah and Israel, as descended from Jacob; but like the two brothers there were many points of opposition between them. See Design C, as showing the general location of Judah and Edom and the likelihood of their being rivals for territory, which is always an unfavourable feature and especially between relatives.

Great Notes of Prophecy. Brief as are these first written prophecies, Obadiah's having only twenty-one verses and Joel's three chapters—a total of seventy-three verses—yet they sound forth great notes that run through all prophecy. Both have the grand key-note idea of the day of the Lord: Obadiah saying, "For the day of the Lord is near upon all the heathen" (verse 15); and Joel, "The day of the Lord is at hand" (1. 15), and "the day of the Lord cometh" (2. 1). Then Obadiah has the idea of the coming of God's kingdom, saying, "And the kingdom shall be the Lord's" (verse 21); while Joel uses the phrase "my holy mountain" (3. 17), a mountain, in Scripture symbolism, meaning a kingdom. P. 714. Joel gives the wonderful promise of the outpouring of the Spirit upon all flesh (2. 28, 29), which Peter showed had its first fulfilment on the day of Pentecost; and it is remarkable that Joel, "coming at the very beginning of written prophecy (B. C. 836), gives the fullest view of the consummation of all written prophecy." P. 930. See page 930 also for the order of events at the end of the Church-age and in the Kingdom-age, as given by Joel.

DESIGN C
OBADIAH AND EDOM

Questions

1. In the reign of what queen in Judah did the ministry of Obadiah occur?

2. During the reign of what king may we place the ministry of Joel?

3. In general, with what two prophets in Israel were Obadiah and Joel in Judah contemporary?

4. What false god made a crisis in both kingdoms?

5. From what neighbouring people was his worship introduced?

6. What woman stood back of this worship in Israel?

7. What is meant by the Remnant?

8. With what neighbouring people is the written prophecy of Obadiah concerned?

9. What two prophetic key-notes are common to Obadiah and Joel?

10. What other wonderful notes of prophecy are given by Joel?

Program 3

AMOS AND HOSEA

The Rugged Prophet of Righteousness. Amos says of himself: "I was an herdman and a gatherer of sycomore fruit: and the Lord took me as I followed the flock, and the Lord said unto me, 'Go, prophecy unto my people Israel'" (Amos 7. 14, 15). At the opening of his prophecy we learn that he was of Tekoa, which is in the rough hill country of Judea, six miles south of Bethlehem. We can thus picture him as a rugged countryman, living with his flock of sheep and at the same time caring for the sycamore trees, which produced a harsh fig needing to be pinched in order to ripen. Here, then, we have the case of Amos, a plain peasant out of Judah, responding to the divine call and "prophesying (B. C. 776–763) in the Northern Kingdom during the reign of Jeroboam II, an able but idolatrous king who brought his kingdom to the zenith of its power." P. 934. And the key-note of his written prophecy is righteousness. "Let judgment run down as waters, and righteousness as a mighty stream" (Amos 5. 24).

His Strength and Courage. The ministry of Amos seems to have been largely at Bethel, just over the line from the Southern Kingdom, but where the idolatrous calf worship centred, which was probably fostered by Jeroboam II so as to hold his people away from the temple worship at Jerusalem. As Amos goes on with his faithful and searching words in this

DESIGN D—AMOS AND EIGHT PEOPLES

[within map: Names in Amos, chs. 1, 2, show that his prophetic vision sees: 1. Syria; 2. Philistia; 3. Phoenicia; 4. Edom; 5. Ammon; 6. Moab; 7. Judah; 8. Israel]

centre of the proud and luxurious life of Israel, he is practically charged by Amaziah, the priest of the calf worship, with being a disturber, and is given this request: "O thou seer, go, flee thee away into the land of Judah, and there eat bread, and prophesy there: but prophesy not again any more at Bethel: for it is the king's chapel, and it is the king's court" (Amos 7. 12, 13). But although accused to King Jeroboam, Amos has the strength and courage to keep his post and be true to his message.

His Outlook. Design D will show that Amos, in his first chapter, looks at six peoples that lie on the borders of Israel and Judah; and then, in his second chapter, looks at Judah and Israel. In his other seven chapters he continues to deal with "the whole family" of God's chosen people (Amos 3. 1, 13). The judgments on Judah and Israel were fulfilled as to Judah in the seventy years' captivity; as to Israel in the world-wide dispersion which still continues. The expressions "whole family" and "house of Jacob" in the verses last referred to evidently give the prophecy an application to both Israel and Judah. Jehovah's controversy with the Gentile cities mentioned in the first chapter of Amos is brief: "I will send a fire." But His covenant people had been brought into the place of privilege and so of responsibility, and the Lord's indictment in the chapters 2 to 9 is detailed and unsparing. P. 935.

Period of Hosea. Hosea was a contemporary of Amos in Israel, and of Isaiah and Micah in Judah, and his ministry continued after the first, or Assyrian, captivity of the Northern Kingdom (2 Ki. 15. 29). P. 921.

His Message. Israel is Jehovah's adulterous wife, repudiated, but ultimately to be purified and restored. This thought may be summed up in his two words, Lo-ammi—"not my people," and Ammi—"my people." P. 921.

Not the New Testament Relation. This relationship is not to be confounded with that of the Church to Christ. The New Testament speaks of the church as a virgin espoused to one husband (2 Cor. 11. 1, 2); which could never be said of an adulterous wife, restored in grace. Israel is then to be the restored and forgiven wife of Jehovah; the Church the virgin wife of the Lamb: Israel Jehovah's earthly wife: the Church the Lamb's heavenly bride. P. 922.

Class Feature. Under the direction of the leader the class may read Hosea 2. 19, and consider "lovingkindness" as the key-note of Hosea as a prophet.

Questions

1. Where did Amos live before he became a prophet?
2. In which kingdom did he have his prophetic ministry?
3. Under what king?
4. Who wished him to retire from Bethel to Judah?
5. What word gives the key-note of Amos?
6. Can you give an idea of his outlook?
7. What was the period of Hosea?
8. What two words give the essence of his message?
9. What distinguishes the New Testament relation of the Church and Christ as contrasted with that of Israel and Jehovah?
10. What word gives the key-note of Hosea?

Program 4

JONAH

Historical Character. The historical character of the man Jonah is vouched for by Jesus Christ (Matt. 12. 39–41). Our Lord also asserts that Jonah's preservation in the great fish was a "sign" or type of His own entombment and resurrection. Both are miraculous and both are equally credible. In 2 Ki. 14, 25 there is recorded the fulfillment of a prophecy by Jonah. The man himself was a bigoted son of Israel, unwilling to testify to a Gentile city, and angry when God spared it. P. 943.

What He Foreshadows. As a type he foreshadows the Hebrew people out of their own land; a trouble to the Gentiles, yet witnessing to them; cast out by them, but miraculously preserved; in their future deepest distress calling upon Jehovah-Saviour, and finding deliverance, and then becoming missionaries to the Gentiles (Zech. 8. 7–23). P. 943.

Widening Sense of Divine Love. As a whole the book of Jonah has risen to a new place of honour as it is seen to contain in the Old Testament revelation a disclosure of the outreaching of divine love toward the Gentile world. God's ancient people needed to have the truth brought home to them that His purpose of salvation was not exhausted or finished when it reached them. The message of the book of Jonah was a missionary challenge to the Israelites. Were they willing to take the knowledge of God—His law against sin and also His forgiving mercy—outside themselves to the great Gentile nations? Jonah showed that he, one Israelite, was not willing to go as a missionary to one nation, Assyria.

Class Feature. The leader may consider with the class whether our Christian world is missionary in its attitude toward the black, brown, and yellow races, or even toward the Hebrew people to whom originally this lesson of Jonah was given.

Jonah Disobedient. There was a basis for Jonah's objection to going to Nineveh, for the Assyrians had treated the Jewish people most cruelly in war. Why should it be necessary to bring them to repentance? Jonah will avoid such a task. Design E shows how extreme is his spirit of disobedience. He takes no mild or neutral stand by remaining in Gath-hepher. He starts from this, his native place, near Nazareth in the Northern Kingdom, to go to Tarshish, the utmost bound of the west in his day. It would take him to the port of Joppa in the opposite direction from Nineveh, and then by ship over two thousand miles through the whole length of the Mediterranean, out through the Pillars of Hercules at Gibraltar to Tarshish on the Atlantic coast lands of Spain.[1] It is as if a man whom God asked to go as a missionary to Patagonia should decide to flee to Circle City, Alaska.

Afflictive and Corrective Providence. Man is no match for God, who, when His servant specializes in disobedience, uses special means to circumvent him. "To faith, and to true science, miracle is what might be expected of divine love for good in a physically and morally disordered universe." P. 944.

Jonah Obedient. When Jonah turns from his own way, God forgives and recommissions him; and Design E shows his route of seven hundred miles of land journeying to Nineveh, and the same route in returning to Gath-hepher. His great work is performed, and the far-spread Gentile city is saved. The angry prophet, on his return route, is gently made to

[1] See Inset, Design E.

94

know the feelings and purposes of the All-Father, extending above and around the limitations and weaknesses of His human instruments, whom nevertheless He condescends to use. Jonah even typifies Christ as the sent One, raised from the dead, and carrying salvation to the Gentiles. Pp. 943-945.

Questions

1. Under what king of Israel did Jonah prophesy, according to the record in 2 Kings 14. 25?

2. Had Jonah some ground for being unwilling to preach to the Ninevites?

3. Can you mention two or three points as to what Jonah typifies?

4. Was God's choice of Israel meant to end with them?

5. Is God's ultimate aim the same in our being chosen as His children?

6. What facts show that Jonah was extreme in his disobedience?

7. Where and at about what distance from Palestine was Tarshish located?

8. About how far did the prophet journey to reach Nineveh?

9. What was the result of his preaching?

10. What special disclosure of God is shown in His closing steps with the prophet?

DESIGN E—JONAH DISOBEDIENT AND OBEDIENT

Program 5

ISAIAH AND MICAH

Greatness of Isaiah and His Prophecy. In Isaiah the man and in his writings as given in the Scriptures we reach the summit of the range of Old Testament prophecy. That the book of Isaiah stands first among the prophetic books results from the rule of putting the longer writings first, but in this case Isaiah deserves to stand first. It is akin to the Gospels in its Messianic tone. P. 711. That we may feel its surprising variety of subjects and soaring sweep of truth we may review Program 3 of Course I, where it is treated as one of the leading books of the Bible.[1] Let us now note a few other points.

DESIGN F—(A) ISAIAH'S WORLD (B) TWO ROUTES
APPROACHING JERUSALEM

Isaiah's World. Section (A) of Design F indicates the wide geographical outlook of Isaiah. The word "Sinim" (Isa. 49. 12) is supposed to refer to a people of the far East, perhaps the Chinese. P. 957. See Design F, Section (A), Inset.

Contemporary Kings. Isaiah, in his first verse, defines his period as "In the days of Uzziah, Jotham, Ahaz, and Hezekiah, Kings of Judah." This era marks the ripe, culminating stage of the Southern Kingdom, when it showed the greatest strength and culture, and when the exalted influence and leadership of Isaiah was exerted for forty-two years.

Paired with Micah. The duality of prophetic ministry seems to continue as we proceed through this Course, and we find that there is a vital connection between the great Isaiah, identified with the city of Jerusalem, and Micah, a more humble village prophet of Moresheth-gath, situated in the low hills about twenty miles southwest of the capital. Almost the exact words of Micah 4. 1–3 are also given in Isa. 2. 2–4. Perhaps the plain man from the hills first uttered these wonderful words in the street of Jerusalem, and Isaiah, hearing them, was led to incorporate them also in this prophecy.

March of the Assyrians. We may note that Micah, in his first chapter, by the succession of places named in verses 9–15, gives the route or line of march of the Assyrian army in its approach to Jerusalem. P. 946. See Design F, Section (B), 1.

---

[1] Pages 18, 19 of these Courses.

96

March of the Man of Sin. On the other hand, in a plan of approach more directly from the north, Isaiah, in 10. 28–32, by a succession of names, indicates the route or line of march of the Beast or Man of Sin directing "the approach of the Gentile hosts to the battle of Armageddon," p. 723, shortly before the Kingdom-age which is still in the future. See Design **F**, Section (B), 2.

Many "Pattern" Elements. More fully than any other written prophecy the book of Isaiah gives the great elements that make up the "mould of predictive prophecy" p. 711, or the "pattern of prophecy," as it has been called in the General View of this Course.

Class Feature. Among elements in Isaiah and Micah the Messianic is the supreme one; and the leader and class may well survey this, as fully as time permits. See pages 716, 717, 747–750, 753, 760, 765, 949, 950.

Other Elements in Isaiah and Micah. Israel and the Remnant, the day of the Lord, the Kingdom, are some of the other features, with helpful points on pages 722, 723, 948–950.

Questions

1. Why may Isaiah be called the summit of prophecy?
2. Can you indicate the general boundary of Isaiah's world?
3. What four kings of Judah were contemporary with Isaiah?
4. About how long was his prophetic period?
5. How do you compare Micah with Isaiah?
6. What proves that the two had vital touch with each other?
7. In what chapter does Micah give the route of the Assyrian army approaching Jerusalem?
8. In what chapter does Isaiah show the route of the final Gentile approach?
9. What is the supreme element in Isaiah's pattern of prophecy?
10. Can you give other elements of the pattern in these two prophets?

Program 6

NAHUM, ZEPHANIAH, HABAKKUK, AND JEREMIAH

General Setting of Nahum. In the first verse of his prophecy Nahum is called "The Elkoshite," which may mean that he was a native of a small place called Elkosh located in the territory of Judah southwest of Jerusalem on the road to Gaza. As to date he comes in the interval between Isaiah and Jeremiah. Design G, Section (A).

His Message. Nahum has but one subject—the destruction of Nineveh. Under the preaching of Jonah the city and king had turned to God. But in the time of Nahum, more than a century later, the city had wholly apostasized from God. Nineveh stands in Scripture as the representative or symbol of apostate *religious* Gentiledom, as Babylon represents the confusion into which the Gentile *political* world-system has fallen. P. 952.

Zephaniah's Ministry. Zephaniah was a descendant of King Hezekiah, being a contemporary of Jeremiah and exercising his ministry during the reign of Josiah. It was a time of revival, largely inspired by the book of the law which had been freshly discovered. Nevertheless, the Exile was impending, and Zephaniah points out the moral state of Judah which made its downfall inevitable. P. 957; Design G, Section (A).

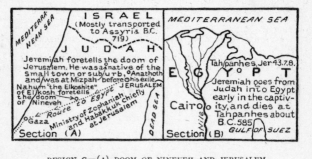

DESIGN G—(A) DOOM OF NINEVEH AND JERUSALEM
(B) JEREMIAH'S LAST DAYS IN EGYPT

Date of Habakkuk. Of Habakkuk himself nothing is known, and there are no allusions in his prophecy which would enable us to determine his exact period. It seems most probable from his description of the Chaldeans (Hab. 1. 6–11), which is the term used by the prophets of this period of the people of the New Babylonian or Chaldean Empire, that he prophesied in the later years of Josiah. P. 955; Design G, Section (A).

His Message. To Habakkuk the character of Jehovah was revealed in terms of the highest spirituality. He alone of the prophets was more concerned that the holiness of Jehovah should be vindicated than that Israel should escape chastisement. Written just upon the eve of the captivity, the prophecy of Habakkuk was God's testimony to Himself as against both idolatry and pantheism. P. 955.

Evangelic Word "Faith." The great evangelic word or phrase, "the just shall live by his faith" (Hab. 2. 4), opens life to faith alone, and

98

makes possible not only the salvation of the Gentiles during the dispersion of Israel among the nations, but also makes possible a believing remnant in Israel while the nation as such is in blindness and unbelief. P. 956.

Class Feature. Let the leader and class trace out and discuss the far-reaching influence of this statement about faith: (1) for Jew and Gentile, Rom. 1. 17; (2) for Gentiles, Gal. 3. 11–14; (3) for Hebrews, Heb. 10. 38; (4) for Luther and the Reformation, etc. P. 956.

Period of Jeremiah. The prophet Jeremiah began his ministry in the thirteenth year of Josiah, about sixty years after Isaiah's death. Zephaniah and Habakkuk were contemporaries of his earlier ministry, and Daniel of his later. After the death of Josiah the kingdom of Judah hastened to its end in the Babylonian captivity. Jeremiah remained in the land ministering to the poor Remnant until they went into Egypt, whither he also went, and where he died early in the seventy years' captivity. Prophesying before and in the early part of the exile of Judah, he connects the pre-exilic prophets with Ezekiel and Daniel, the prophets of the exile. P. 772; Design G, Sections (A) and (B).

Jeremiah's Messages. The messages or sermons of Jeremiah may be said to have greater definiteness of time and occasion than those of any other of the major prophets; as can be seen in the subheads throughout. They include: the Babylonian captivity; the return after seventy years; the world-wide dispersion; the remnant; the final regathering; the day of judgment on the Gentile powers; the kingdom-age. P. 772.

Questions

1. Where probably is the hamlet located that causes Nahum to be called "The Elkoshite"?
2. Between what two prophets does he come as to date?
3. Against what city is his prophecy directed?
4. What discovery and revival form the background of the prophecy of Zephaniah?
5. In the later years of what king may we place the prophecy of Habakkuk?
6. What element of God's character does he bring out?
7. What evangelic phrase having wonderful influence on subsequent religious thought is found in Habakkuk?
8. What two great divisions of prophecy are connected by the ministry of Jeremiah?
9. Can you name three places, apart from Jerusalem, related to his life history?
10. What are some of the topics covered by his messages?

Program 7

EZEKIEL AND DANIEL

Extension of Dual Feature. The duality of prophetic ministry still marks this Course, although Programs 4, 6, and 8 are apparent exceptions. Yet in these, while Jonah stands alone in Program 4, he can be paired with Nahum in Program 6 as both are concerned with Nineveh, and of the three left in Program 6; Zephaniah can be associated with Jeremiah. Then, in Program 8 Haggai and Zechariah go together, thus leaving only Habakkuk and Malachi as most individual and separate; and it is easy to relate them by their common stressing of God's holiness. Thus it will help to hold the entire procession of the Old Testament prophets in our thought if we arrange the eighteen men in nine pairs.

DUAL ARRANGEMENT OF THE PROPHETS	
Elijah and Elisha	Jeremiah and Zephaniah
Obadiah and Joel	Ezekiel and Daniel
Amos and Hosea	Haggai and Zechariah
Isaiah and Micah	Habakkuk and Malachi
Jonah and Nahum	

Two Prophets Set Apart. The two prophets Ezekiel and Daniel are especially set apart from the others and closely united in several respects. In the first place, they were both among the people of Judah transported to Babylon, although they may not have gone in the same company of captives. Ezekiel was carried away to Babylon between the first and

DESIGN H—EZEKIEL AT TELABIB.   ROUTE OF DANIEL TO BABYLON

final deportations of Judah. P. 840. From the first chapter of Daniel it is clear that he as a child or youth had also passed over the route from Jerusalem to Babylon. P. 898; Design H. In the second place, they both prophesied out of the land; that is, they were prophets of the Exile.

In the third place, as is stated in the latter part of the Panoramic View, while the general line of the writing prophets were inspired preachers, and their prophetical books consist of sermons with brief connecting explanatory passages, the two prophetical books are of a different character and are largely apocalyptic. Last page of Panoramic View. As such, they follow the method of symbol and vision. P. 840. In the fourth place, we should note that, unlike the pre-exilic prophets, they sound forth the voice of Jehovah to "the whole house of Israel." P. 840.

General Aim of Ezekiel. Speaking broadly, the purpose of Ezekiel's ministry is to keep before the generation born in exile the national sins which had brought Israel so low; and to sustain the faith of the exiles by predictions of national restoration, of the execution of justice on their oppressors, and of national glory under the future Davidic monarchy. P. 840.

Class Feature. Let the class, using Design H, in thought try to picture Ezekiel as located not far from Babylon at Telabib, a settlement of Jewish captives on "the river of Chebar" (Ezek. 1. 1), which is thought to be a canal or water-course derived from the Euphrates.

Daniel's Life and Work. Daniel was of royal or princely descent. For his rank and comeliness he was trained for palace service, where he achieved a record of singular purity and usefulness. His long life extended from Nebuchadnezzar to Cyrus. He was a contemporary of Jeremiah and Ezekiel, of Ezra and Zerubbabel, and the events recorded in his prophecy cover a period of seventy-three years. P. 898.

The Book of Daniel. The first chapter is an introduction, giving the early personal history of Daniel. Chapters 2 to 4 relate the visions of Nebuchadnezzar and their results. In Program 2 of Course IV, on "Christ in the Prophets," the image and the stone cut out of the mountain, as seen by Nebuchadnezzar in one of these dreams or visions have been explained.[1] Chapters 5 and 6 continue the personal history of Daniel under Belshazzar and Darius. The remaining chapters, 7 to 12, contain the visions of Daniel himself and their interpretation. As a general summary it may be said that "his vision sweeps the whole course of Gentile world-rule to its end in catastrophe, and to the setting up of the Messianic kingdom." P. 898.

Questions

1. If we fully arrange the prophets in sets of two, what prophet may be placed with Jonah and why?
2. What prophet can be associated with Jeremiah?
3. What one with Malachi?
4. Can you give some of the respects in which Ezekiel and Daniel are closely united?
5. What characterizes the style of apocalyptic writings?
6. On what canal or water-course was Telabib, the place of residence of Ezekiel, located?
7. To what place were Daniel and other youths of Judah assigned?
8. With what kings was Daniel brought in contact?
9. How many years are covered by the book of Daniel?
10. What two topics summarize his prophetic vision?

[1] Page 73 of these Courses.

Program 8

HAGGAI, ZECHARIAH, AND MALACHI

Return from Captivity. The return of Jews from their captivity, being chiefly offspring of dwellers in the kingdom of Judah who had been taken to Babylon seventy years earlier, was in two main companies that traversed the route of twelve hundred miles up through Mesopotamia to Haran and Carchemish and then down through Syria because the desert prevented their going west or slightly southwest from Babylon to Jerusalem. Their general course is seen in Design J, Section (A). The order of the restoration with the several leaders was as follows: 1. The return of the first detachment under Zerubbabel and Joshua, B. C. 536 (Ezra 1–6); 2. the expedition of Ezra, B. C. 458, seventy-eight years later (Ezra 7–10); 3. the commission of Nehemiah, B. C. 444, fourteen years after the expedition of Ezra (Neh. 2. 1–5). P. 530. Those returning with Zerubbabel numbered 42,360 and their male and female servants 7,337 or a total of 49,697 (Ezra 2. 64, 65). With Ezra there returned a company that numbered nearly 1,800 males (Ezra 8. 1–20), and these, with their wives and "little ones" (Ezra 8. 21), would probably amount to two and a half times that number, or a total of 4,500. However, as these did not arrive in the restored Persian Province of Judah until seventy-eight years after the first company came, we are to think of the 50,000 under Zerubbabel and their natural increase through one or two generations as the community to whom Haggai and Zechariah ministered. The 50,000 arrived at Jerusalem, according to Ussher, in B. C. 536, and he dates the beginning of the ministry of the two prophets in B. C. 520, or sixteen years after the return; and he extends the prophecy of the book of Zechariah through thirty-five years until B. C. 487.

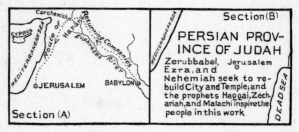

DESIGN J—(A) THE RETURN.   (B) THE REBUILDERS

Mission of Post-exilic Prophets. The task of Haggai, and Malachi was to hearten, rebuke, and instruct the feeble and divided remnant, after the return, in their work of reconstruction at Jerusalem and throughout the Persian Province of Judah. Not only were the city walls and the temple to be rebuilt, but the very history and religion of the Jewish people were to be kept alive among these new settlers in their home-land. P. 962; Design J, Section (B).

Haggai and Jehovah's House. The theme of Haggai, is the unfinished temple, and his mission is to admonish and encourage the builders. The prophet calls the old men who remembered Solomon's temple to witness to the new generation how greatly that structure exceeded the present in magnificence. P. 963.

102

Prophecy of Zechariah. There is much of symbolism in Zechariah, but these difficult passages are readily interpreted in the light of the whole body of related prophecy. The great Messianic passages are, upon comparison with the other prophecies of the kingdom, perfectly clear. Both advents of Christ are in Zechariah's prophecy (Zech. 9. 9, to be connected with Matt. 21. 1–11, and Zech. 14. 3, 4). More than Haggai or Malachi, Zechariah gives the mind of God about the Gentile world-powers surrounding the restored remnant. He has given them their authority, and will hold them to account; the test, as always, being their treatment of Israel. P. 965.

Closing Message of Malachi. In the year B. C. 397, as reckoned by Ussher, we reach the last prophetic utterance to the restored remnant, and find that Malachi's message unfolds three subjects: the love of Jehovah, the sins of the priests and of the people, and the day of the Lord. As a whole, he gives the moral judgment of God on the remnant restored by His grace under Ezra and Nehemiah. God has established His house among the people of Judah, but their worship is formal and insincere. P. 980.

Class Feature. Let the leader and class exalt the fact that prophecy consists largely of "inspired sermons," p. 773, and ask not only for ministers but for each believing soul God-imparted truth, to be used as the Spirit may direct. There may be closing prayers for "such an effusion of the Spirit as the prophets described." P. 982.

Questions

1. What made so long a detour necessary in the route between Jerusalem and Babylon?
2. Under what leader did the first detachment return to the province of Judah?
3. As a round total, about how many did it number?
4. In what year B. C., according to Ussher, did the ministry of Haggai and Zechariah begin?
5. What is the special theme of the prophecy of Haggai?
6. What marked features do we find in the prophecy of Zechariah?
7. What is the date of the return under Ezra?
8. About how many may we estimate his expedition numbered?
9. What three subjects does Malachi unfold?
10. At what date, according to Ussher, was the last Old Testament book of prophecy written?

25 Review and Test Questions on Course V
(For directions see Note on page 29)

1. What type of men were the prophets? P. 86.
2. Who were the two non-writing prophets? P. 88.
3. What quality was needed in Elijah? P. 88.
4. What qualities mark Elisha? P. 88.
5. What alien cult in Judah was overcome by Obadiah and Joel, much as Elijah and Elisha overcame it in Israel? P. 90.
6. With what neighboring land was Obadiah concerned? P. 90.
7. What prophecy of Joel did Peter quote at Pentecost? P. 91.
8. In which of the two kingdoms were Amos and Hosea prophets? P. 92.
9. Can you give the key-note word for Amos? P. 92.
10. What is the key-note word for Hosea? P. 93.
11. What new assertion of divine love appears in God's statements to Jonah? P. 94.
12. Can you show how extreme Jonah was in his purpose of disobedience? P. 94.
13. What special barrier was in the way of his accepting a mission to the Assyrians? P. 94.
14. Can you name one or more of the kings of Judah in Isaiah's time? P. 96.
15. What is thought to be the country called "Sinim" in Isaiah? P. 96.
16. What prophet in a village southwest of Jerusalem is associated with Isaiah? P. 96.
17. From what king of Judah was Zephaniah, the prophet, descended? P. 98.
18. What declaration about faith, in the prophecy of Habakkuk, came to Luther in Rome? Pp. 98, 99.
19. What terrible event for the kingdom of Judah occurred during the ministry of Jeremiah? P. 99.
20. What was the period of Ezekiel and Daniel, setting them apart from others? P. 100.
21. By what word can we designate the style of their writings? P. 101.
22. In what city did Daniel carry through his many years of service? P. 101.
23. What is the theme of Haggai's prophecy? P. 102.
24. What is the outlook of Zechariah as respects Christ and the surrounding nations? P. 103.
25. About what is the date of Malachi, the last of the Old Testament prophets? P. 103.

COURSE VI

PERSONAL DIVINE LIFE

General View

PROGRESS TOWARD COMPLETE CHRISTIAN CHARACTER

---

1. Discipline and Teaching.
2. Knowledge and Guidance.
3. By-path Warnings.
4. Prayer.

5. Service.
6. Fellowship and Worship.
7. Union with God and Fulness of the Spirit.

Large Place of Personality. When we attempt to grasp the significance of the Bible and the type of life which is exalted therein, it would be hard to say where personality as a factor entering into divine revelation and spiritual life begins and ends. At the very threshold of Scripture, personality takes on large meaning in the account of the creation of man. He is at the summit of all that was made, and likeness of God his Creator is stamped upon his nature. God has personality, and a part of His image in man is personality. Soul and self-consciousness of a much higher order than those possessed by animals belong to man and tend to distinguish him as a person or individual. P. 5.

Bible Emphasizes the Personal Factor. As we proceed through the legal and historical books of the Old Testament from Genesis to Esther we are almost constantly passing from person to person—from Adam to Seth, from Seth to Enoch, from Enoch to Noah, from Noah to Abraham, and thus onward in their order like so many milestones, with many minor individuals interspersed. The lists of antediluvian patriarchs, of Hebrew founders and tribal heads, of judges, and of kings, form a long and almost unbroken succession. Prophetic characters, like Moses and Samuel, and the recognized list of eighteen prophets considered in Course V, form another succession of persons; and to this may be added a considerable group of other individuals associated with the prophetical books.

Christ the Pivotal Person. Not only the Bible, but all of God's revealing and religious designs relating to mankind centre in Christ as the pivotal Person. Christianity is a religion built about a Person. This is seen in the last paragraph of the Panoramic View, where is stressed "his Person, as 'God manifest in the flesh,'" and in the preview of the Four Gospels, where the main conclusion reached is that "in all alike is revealed one unique Personality." P. 990.

Apostles Complete the Bible. In the person of apostolic workers the New Testament largely finds its inspired writers, who bring the whole Bible to completion. At the same time they are to a prevailing extent the spiritual leaders and saintly exemplars who, in their own individual embodiments of gifts and graces of the Spirit, and in their ministry to the life of believers, build up the mystical body of Christ. Pp. 1008, 1222, 1247, 1253.

Movement Toward Inner Divine Life. The movement of biblical religion is from the mass to the individual, and from things external to the reality and enrichment of inner divine life. The book of Psalms, beyond all other books of the Old Testament, is prized by Christians of to-day because they hear in it the voices of individuals interpreting the moods and movements of the life of God in the soul of man. "The great themes of the Psalms are, Christ, Jehovah, the Law, Creation, the future of Israel, and the exercises of the renewed heart in suffering, in joy, in perplexity. The promises of the Psalms are primarily Jewish, and suited to a people under the law, but are spiritually true in Christian experience also, in the sense that they disclose the mind of God, and the exercises of his heart toward those who are perplexed, afflicted, or cast down." P. 599. However, the Psalms may scarcely appear in this Course, because the experiences of the believer as portrayed in many leading Psalms have previously been drawn out in Program 2 of Course I, and those of Christ in other Psalms in Program 3 of Course IV.[1]

Culmination in the Epistles. The several lines of this Course will naturally find their culmination in the New Testament, where the individual and personal phases of Christian attainment come into their own; and especially in the Epistles, where the inner glories of the life in Christ have their full unfoldment. The transition open to those who pass from a state of nature into their heritage of personal divine life is indicated in Design A.

[1] See pages 16, 17 and 74, 75 of these Courses.

OUT OF GRACE	IN GRACE
1. Man out of grace, under the dominion of sin. P. 195.	1. Man, in grace, having sin's dominion broken. P. 1195.
2. The "natural" man has enmity and aversion toward God. 1263.	2. The spiritual man has love and trust toward God. 1263.
3. The unsaved man without God and without hope in the world. 1251.	3. The saved man has God's favour, and the cheer of faith and hope. 1267.
4. The unregenerate man, "in the flesh," has (1329) whole spirit, soul and body centred in self.	4. The regenerate man, "in the Spirit," has (1355) whole spirit, soul, and body centred in Christ
5. The confirmed evil man abandoned and given up by the Spirit. 1295	5. The confirmed Christ-like man ever more (1149) fully set apart for God by the Spirit.
6. Death viewed with callousness, dread, fear or terror. Heb 2:15.	6. Death viewed as a "sleep" in anticipation of a joyous resurrection. 1299
7. In second resurrection, after the millennium. 1228	7. In first resurrection, before the millennium. 1228.
8. Arraigned in the final judgment. 1351	8. Free from the final judgment. 1233.
9. Examined from the books. 1351.	9. Delivered and kept in faith by Christ's advocacy (1136) if accused before God and sifted by Satan
10. Adjudged guilty. 1361.	10. Counted righteous in Christ. 1044.
11. Assigned to the place of punishment. 228.	11. Never subject to jeopardy, since Christ has become our surety. 1133.
12. Second death, eternal separation from God in conscious suffering. 1221, 1351.	12. Secure in eternal blessedness, final and irreversible. 1296.

DESIGN A—HUMANITY OUT OF GRACE AND IN GRACE

Program 1

DISCIPLINE AND TEACHING

At the Childhood Stage. Among the points emphasized at the opening of the Epistle to the Ephesians we note this statement: "The believer's relation to God as a child results from the new birth" (John 1. 12, 13). P. 1250. As in the case of all things that show life and growth we can understand that training or discipline and instruction or teaching are especially required for believers while they are in the childhood stage. This Program, therefore, comes properly at the beginning of our consideration of the subject of personal divine life. Some measure of discipline and teaching may continue during the later periods of such a life, but there can be no question of this cultural, corrective, and educative process being needed by the young disciple. The very word "disciple" implies discipline and teaching.

Analogy of the Race and of Israel. There are analogies that apply to the individual believer in the way that God disciplined and taught both the whole race and then the chosen people, in the childhood of each, as has been recorded in the early books of the Bible. We pass over the example of the race for the present, but concerning Israel God says this: "When Israel was a child, then I loved him, and called my son out of Egypt" (Hos. 12. 1). Incidents of the exodus and of the early wilderness journeyings teem with teaching points. The wilderness was part of the necessary discipline of the redeemed people. The Red Sea, Marah, Elim, and Sinai were God's ways in development and discipline, and have, of necessity, their counterpart in Christian experience. The Red Sea speaks of the cross as that which—death to Christ but life for us—separates us from Egypt, the world (Gal. 6. 14) Marah of God's power to turn untoward things into blessing; Elim of God's power to give rest and refreshment by the way; Sinai of God's holiness and our deep inherent evil, in reality the experience of Romans 7. 24. These episodes were of God's ordering. But not so the later wanderings in the wilderness (Num. 14. 33), which were due wholly to the unbelief of the people at Kadesh-Barnea in doubting and denying that God was able to lead them into the promised land. P. 186. These wanderings will be touched upon in Program 3.

Design B. Design B, Section (A), shows the route of the Israelites from Succoth to Kadesh-Barnea with some of the features and stations mentioned in Numbers 33. 5–19. It represents the period of Divine discipline in the Exodus. Section (B), on the other hand, shows the weary wilderness wanderings and many stations, as given in Numbers 33. 19–35, covering thirty-eight years, while the generation that came out of Egypt slowly died in the desert because, through unbelief and lack of trust in God's power, the people would not go up from Kadesh-Barnea and take possession of Palestine.

Class Feature. Let the leader conduct a brief and informal class conference, considering how far the bitter as well as bright episodes of life, represented by Marah and Elim, are viewed by the members as God's way of discipline and teaching; or how far members may see in them the fruit of unbelief and failure to follow God's leading.

God's Teaching. This theme opens a wide vista. Look at the Introduction to Deuteronomy and the headings of chapters four and five as showing the bearing of Moses' closing teaching in that book. Pp. 216, 220, 222. The festivals were great teaching occasions. P. 156–158. One of the main objects of the inspired Scriptures is "instruction in righteousness." The goal is the "spiritual" man or woman, "Spirit-filled and walking in the Spirit in full communion with God," pp. 1213, 1214.

Questions

1. What experience brings man into relation to God as a child?
2. What is especially appropriate for the believer's childhood stage?
3. In what book of prophecy is Israel spoken of as a child?
4. About what part of the Exodus journey is viewed as a period of discipline in the Divine plan?   P. 186.
5. What does the station Marah signify spiritually?   P. 186.
6. What is the spiritual significance of the station Elim?   P. 186.
7. How are we to regard the thirty-eight years of wilderness wanderings after Israel left Kadesh-Barnea?   P. 186.
8. Can you show how God could use the festivals as teaching occasions?   Pp. 156–158.
9. What is one of the main objects of the Scriptures?
10. What are the highest ways in which God teaches the believer? Pp. 1213, 1297.

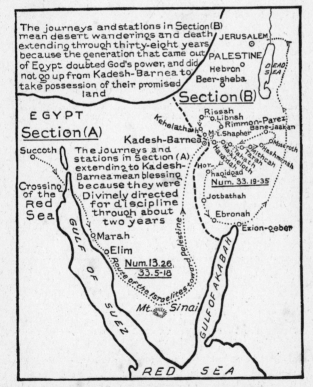

DESIGN B—(A) FRUIT OF DISCIPLINE, LARGER LIFE
(B) FRUIT OF UNBELIEF, DESERT DEATH

Program 2

KNOWLEDGE AND GUIDANCE

A Golden Sequence. Those who are true disciples and who are responsive to the developing influences that come through discipline are rewarded with the golden sequence of a growing enlightenment and understanding, which ripens into full spiritual knowledge. Likewise the fruit of Divine teaching is a steady increase in the faculty of discernment, until presently the believer is conscious that he lives in an atmosphere of spiritual guidance. "I understand more than the ancients," says the Psalmist, "because I keep thy precepts" (Psa. 119. 100). "Thine ears shall hear a word behind thee, saying, This is the way, walk ye in it, when ye turn to the right hand, and when ye turn to the left" (Isa. 30. 21).

Degrees of Knowledge. There are degrees or gradations of knowledge; and it will be found that the books of the inspired Word represent points of view ranged apparently according to man's power of approximation to the Divine thought. God lets man take the truth or fact of His existence and the sifting of His final judgment, and then permits His creature to work out his solution of the problems of life and destiny on that basis. Such, for instance, seems to be the point of view of Ecclesiastes.

"Under the Sun." Ecclesiastes is the book of man "under the sun," reasoning about life; it is the best man can do, with the knowledge that there is a holy God, and that He will bring everything into judgment. The key phrases are "under the sun"; "I perceived"; "I said in my heart." Inspiration sets down accurately what passes, but the conclusions and reasonings are, after all, man's. The final "conclusion" (Eccl. 12. 13) is legal, the best that man apart from redemption can do, and does not anticipate the Gospel. P. 696.

Aspects of Wisdom. The collection of sententious sayings in the book of Proverbs is divine wisdom applied to the earthly conditions of the people of God. But when we come to such a characterization of wisdom as is found in the eighth chapter of Proverbs, we are compelled to say that it is more than the personification of an attribute of God or of the will of God as best for man, and becomes a distinct adumbration of Christ, who, as Paul declares, "is made unto us wisdom." P. 677.

Enlightenment. In the Jewish-Christian Epistles—Hebrews, James, First and Second Peter, and Jude—we have a group of inspired writings differing in important respects from Paul's Epistles. But this difference is in no sense one of conflict but of extension or development. The degree of knowledge obtained by some of those referred to is enlightenment. It is said in Hebrews 6. 4 that these have been "enlightened," and the same word is used in Hebrews 10. 32, and translated "illuminated." It is the solicitude of the writer that these beginners in the way of life should go on to complete knowledge of Christ. P. 1289.

Assurance. Much higher than enlightenment is the gradation of spiritual knowledge noted in Jude, the last of these Jewish-Christian books, which is termed assurance. Assurance is the believer's full conviction that, through the work of Christ alone, received by faith, he is in possession of a salvation in which he will be eternally kept. And this assurance rests only upon the Scripture promises to him who believes. P. 1328.

Class Feature. Let a member of the class present in a brief paper or address the biblical view of the relation of the Holy Spirit to the believer's knowledge and guidance. Pp. 1090, 1136, 1150, 1214, 1250. Follow with class discussion and experience.

"*Full-knowledge.*" In contrast to the claims of the Gnostics of Paul's time to a transcendent knowledge (*gnosis*), he shows that the believer has access to divine revelation which gives "full-knowledge" (*epignosis*, Col. 1. 9, 10; 3. 10). P. 1264. Out of this super-knowledge would come adequate guidance, so that the Colossians would "walk" in Christ, "rooted and built up in Him, and established in the faith" (Col. 2. 7.) The warnings against the pretended "knowledge" of the errorists apply to all extra-biblical forms, doctrines, and customs, and to all ascetic practices. P. 1264.

Questions

1. What are the more permanent things that come as a result of discipline and teaching?
2. How may the fact that there are degrees of spiritual knowledge register itself in the Bible?
3. What two ideas or doctrines are taken for granted as a basis for the reasonings of the book of Ecclesiastes?
4. To what realm do the Proverbs apply?
5. What character is back of the praise of wisdom in the eighth chapter of Proverbs?
6. Which of the Epistles may be called Jewish-Christian?
7. What terms are used in the book of Hebrews for some who are beginners?
8. What higher gradation of spiritual knowledge is noted in the Epistle of Jude?
9. What term in Greek represents the claim of the early Gnostics?
10. What Greek term does Paul use in Colossians over against the Gnostics and what does it mean?

Program 3

BY-PATH WARNINGS

God's Will the True Path. From the beginning of the relation between God and man, the essence of law for man has been God's will. Good has meant obedience, evil disobedience, to the revealed will of God. P. 10. Therefore, all sin is a *by-path* or *error*, a departure from the true path, the will of God. P. 1194.

Warning a Factor in Revelation. Man was created in innocency, placed in a perfect environment, subjected to an absolutely simple test, and warned of the consequence of disobedience. P. 5. Among the purposes sought by inspired Scripture are "reproof" and "correction" (2 Tim. 3. 16). These are nearly equivalent to warning.

General Tendency to Choose By-Paths. The fall was a by-path taken by our first parents; and the early generations went into other by-paths of wickedness and pride that called for the flood and the confusion of tongues. Pp. 8, 10, 18. Lot, in choosing Sodom, chose a by-path; and the destruction of the cities of the plain is the warning attached to such a course. Pp. 22, 30. Esau, in despising the birthright, entered a by-path, and found it impossible to regain the full blessing. In many respects a nobler man, naturally, than Jacob, he was destitute of faith, and despised the birthright because it was a spiritual thing, of value only as there was faith to apprehend it. Pp. 38, 41.

Balaam By-Paths. In the case of Balaam, who was desired by Balak to curse Israel, being first told by God not to respond, and afterward apparently permitted to go (Num. 22. 12, 20), we see in verse twelve God's *directive* will which should have been law to the prophet, and in verse twenty His *permissive* will, which really formed a testing of Balaam. When the prophet went, swayed by the motives of self-will and self-advantage, he entered the by-path of a typical hireling prophet, seeking only to make a market of his gift. This is "the way of Balaam" (2 Pet. 2. 15). The *"doctrine of Balaam"* (Rev. 2. 14) refers to his teaching Balak to corrupt the people whom he could not curse, through the temptation offered by the women of Midian and Moab. Pp. 196, 1332, 1333.

Repeated Apostasy in the Period of the Judges. In the time of the Judges Israel repeatedly took the by-path of evil chiefly by being drawn aside from allegiance to God into the idolatrous ways and gross immoralities of surrounding peoples. The judges were spiritual ancestors of the prophets, and they showed the power of God to use the humblest and most imperfect agents, that the result might redound to His glory. P. 289.

By-Paths in the Period of Monarchy. In the books of Samuel, Kings, and Chronicles we find that by-paths from God's thought and order were taken by many of the kings. This was especially true of Saul before the kingdom was divided, when he departed from the divine directions and then proposed to make adjustment by abundant sacrificial offerings. The record would seem to establish the fact that more than half the monarchs of Judah as well as Israel were guilty in one way or another of turning into by-paths of self-seeking, perverseness, idolatry, misrule, or more extreme transgression; and as a consequence there came repeated warnings from the prophets and in the end the captivities of both kingdoms, so that we read: "The failure of Israel under the Palestinian Covenant," in the Judges and Monarchy periods, "brought the judgment of the Captivities." P. 16. Again, we see this conclusion: "The religious state of the people, even at the best, is described in Isaiah, chapter 1–5." P. 490. The book

112

of Jeremiah, also, is almost wholly a continued ministry of warning. See statements, pp. 784, 787.

Applied to Personal Life. Paul makes many of the early Old Testament by-paths warning examples, saying: "Now these things were our examples," that we should not desire evil things; and also, surveying the penalties, he says: "Now all these things happened unto them for ensamples: and they are written for our admonition" (1 Cor. 10. 6, 11).

Class Feature. Let the class seek to make practical use of the by-path idea, asking whether, on the one hand, there is not too much "legalism," as a New Testament by-path, and, on the other hand, not enough "inlawing" of ourselves to Christ, pp. 1243–1245, in our personal divine life. Note that St. John uses "commandments" in the general sense of the divine will, however revealed, and especially of the law of Christ. P. 1337.

Questions

1. What forms our true path for personal divine life?
2. Why may sin be viewed as a by-path?
3. What purposes of Scripture show that it is meant to warn against sin, as a part of its aim?
4. What early tendencies of the race may be viewed as by-paths?
5. Can you name individuals in early Hebrew history who chose by-paths?
6. What form of by-path is represented by Balaam?
7. What type of by-path is common in the period of the Judges and the Monarchy?
8. What word may best designate the by-path taken by King Saul in the matter of the Amalekites?
9. What terms might be applied to the by-path courses of the Northern or Southern Kingdom?
10. What is meant when "legalism" is regarded as a by-path which Christians are now liable to enter?

Program 4

PRAYER

Old Testament and New. Prayer in the Old Testament is in contrast with prayer in the New Testament in two respects: First, in the Old Testament the basis of prayer is a covenant of God, or an appeal to His character as merciful, gracious, and the like. In the New Testament the basis is the relationship between the believer as child and God as Father. Second, a comparison, for example, of the prayers of Moses and Paul, will show that one is praying for an earthly people whose dangers and blessings are earthly; the other for a heavenly people whose dangers and blessings are spiritual. P. 957.

Other Old Testament Examples. Along with the case of Moses we may place several other prayers indicated in the Old Testament, showing that they have earthly considerations as their chief aim. In the eighteenth chapter of Genesis there is the intercessory prayer of Abraham, asking that, should any considerable number of righteous persons be found in Sodom and Gomorrah, such persons may avail to deliver these cities from destruction. Solomon's notable prayer at the dedication of the temple, as given in Kings and Chronicles, encompasses chiefly the earthly fortune of Israelites as they turn their faces toward the sanctuary in their supplications. Pp. 397–399; 494–496. Nehemiah's prayer had in view the rebuilding of the walls of Jerusalem. P. 541.

Approach to the Gospel Experience. David's penitential prayer, as given in the Fifty-first Psalm, closely approximates the Gospel attitude and movement, and shows in its successive steps the elements of experience of a sinning saint who comes back to full communion and service. The steps are: (1) sin thoroughly judged before God; (2) forgiveness and cleansing through the blood; (3) cleansed; (4) Spirit-filled for joy and power; (5) service; (6) worship; (7) zeal for the blessing of Zion. P. 623.

New Testament Basis. In the Sermon on the Mount Christ announces the filial relationship as the new basis of prayer. The believer is a child of God through the new birth. The clear revelation of this fact at once establishes the reasonableness of prayer; and the argument from the apparent uniformity of nature is shattered. God is more than Creator, bringing a universe into being, and establishing laws for it; more than a decree-maker determining future events by an eternal fiat. P. 1089.

The Divine Family. Above all this is the divine family for whom the universe with its laws exists: "When ye pray, say, Our Father." What God habitually does in the material universe concerns the reverent investigator of that universe. What He may do in His own family concerns Him, and is matter for divine promise and revelation. Science, which deals only with natural phenomena, cannot intrude there. P. 1089.

New Testament Summary. Christ's law of prayer may be thus summarized: (1) He grounds prayer upon relationship, and reveals God as freely charging Himself with all responsibilities, as His heart glows with all the affections of a Father toward all who believe on Jesus Christ. Prayer, therefore, is a child's petition to an all-wise, all-loving, and all-powerful Father-God. (2) In the so-called Lord's prayer Christ gives an incomparable model for all prayer. It teaches that right prayer begins with worship; puts the interest of the kingdom before merely personal interest; accepts beforehand the Father's will, whether to grant or withhold; and petitions for present need, leaving the future to the Father's care and love. (3) Prayer to be definite; and (4) importunate, that is, undiscouraged by delayed answers. Pp. 1089, 1090.

Christ's Prayer of Intercession. Christ's great intercessory prayer in the seventeenth chapter of the Gospel of John has seven petitions: (1) that Jesus may be glorified as the Son who has glorified the Father; (2) for restoration to the eternal glory; (3) for the safety of believers from (a) the world, (b) the evil one; (4) for the sanctification of believers; (5) for the spiritual unity of believers; (6) that the world may believe; (7) that believers may be with Him in heaven to behold and share His glory. P. 1139.

Class Feature. Let the leader intimately bring the class in prayer before the Father in the name of Christ. Give opportunity for very free and voluntary experiences in prayer if time permits.

Questions

1. Can you state how the basis of Old Testament prayer contrasts with that in the New Testament?
2. What realm of being is emphasized in Old Testament prayers and what in the New?
3. Can you apply this distinction to the prayer of Abraham concerning Sodom and Gomorrah?
4. What steps of restoration of a sinning saint inspires the prayer of David in the Fifty-first Psalm?
5. What relationship does Christ present as our prayer basis?
6. Why cannot science intrude at this point?
7. In the Lord's prayer what place has worship?
8. How do we estimate the kingdom as compared with personal interest?
9. What do we grant as to the Father's will?
10. What does Jesus ask in His intercessory prayer for our personal divine life?

Program 5

SERVICE

An Essential. In no case does personal divine life attain its true objective and follow the pattern formed by the hand of infinite Love until it yields some measure of service. Acceptable service has back of it a heart that is right with God; but when this condition is met service can exhibit boundless variety. Its most precious effects often come forth from lives unaware that they are rendering service. It is like a well-spring over-flowing. In the preceding Program we may note that when David's communion with God was restored, when he was cleansed and Spirit-filled at once and inevitably there came forth as item (5) "Service." P. 623.

Rod, Hand, Heart. When Moses was about to enter into service for Israel, God gave him profound lessons through the medium of the rod in his hand and the placing of his hand in his bosom as is shown in the fourth chapter of Exodus. The heart ("bosom") stands for what we *are,* the hand for what we *do.* What we are, that ultimately we do. The two signs, rod and hand, speak of preparation for service: 1. consecration—our capacity taken up for God; 2. the hand that holds the rod of God's power must be a cleansed hand swayed by a new heart. P. 74.

Joshua's Favorite Word. The word "serve" or "served" occurs fifteen times in the last chapter of the book of Joshua, and chiefly in Joshua's closing address. It is likely that his greatest service to his people was the reality back of his assertion, when he said: "As for me and my house, we will serve the Lord" (Josh. 24. 15).

"Ruth Serving." Among the attractive and stimulating brief books of the Old Testament, one must see that Ruth holds a high place. Its four divisions are: Ruth deciding, Ruth serving, Ruth resting, Ruth rewarded; and we realize that the one which interprets most perfectly her character is "Ruth serving." P. 316.

Queenly Service. A second minor book of the Old Testament enshrines the queenly service of Esther, another woman whose influence has been far-reaching in Jewish history. Mordecai called her to act a great part when he said: "Who knoweth whether thou art come to the kingdom for such a time as this?" (Esth. 4. 14) She proved equal to the emergency, and we have the action that is worthy to be entitled "the courage of Esther." P. 562.

Range of Christ's Service. In the Psalms especially Christ is seen in His varied service. As Priest He offers Himself in sacrifice, and, in resurrection, as the Priest-Shepherd, ever living to make intercession. As Prophet He proclaims the name of Jehovah as Father. As King He fulfils the Davidic Covenant and restores alike the dominion of man over creation, and of the Father over all. P. 658.

A Service Contrast. In a passage of the Song of Solomon, we see the bride, representing the church or the disciple, satisfied with her washed feet, while the Bridegroom, His "head filled with dew," and His "locks with the drops of the night," is toiling for others. The state of the bride is not one of sin, but of neglect of service. She is preoccupied with the graces and perfections which she has in Christ through the Spirit. It is mysticism, unbalanced by the activities of the Christian warfare. Her feet are washed, her hands drop with sweet-smelling myrrh; but He has gone on, and now she must seek Him. P. 707.

Fruit. As we come to the New Testament we perceive that "fruit" while it has some relation to character, for the most part carries a greatly enlarged and enriched conception of service. There are three conditions

115

of the fruitful life: cleansing, abiding, obedience. P. 1136. There are also three degrees in fruit-bearing: "fruit," "more fruit," "much fruit" (John 15. 5, 8). As we bear "much fruit" the Father is glorified in us. The minor moralities and graces of Christianity are often imitated, but never the ninefold "fruit" of Gal. 5. 22, 23. P. 1137.

Divine Gifts for Service. While, in 1 Cor. 12. 8–28, the Spirit is seen as enduing the members of the body of Christ with spiritual gifts or enablements for a varied service, we find that in Eph. 4. 11–16 certain Spirit-endued men, namely, apostles, prophets, evangelists, pastors, and teachers, are themselves the gifts whom the glorified Christ bestows upon His body the church. P. 1253.

Paul as a Heavenly Prince. The brief letter to Philemon is of priceless value as a teaching 1. in practical righteousness; 2. in Christian brotherhood; 3. in Christian courtesy; 4. in the law of love. P. 1286. Here toilworn Paul, a prisoner at Rome, appears a heavenly prince in his service to a lowly slave convert, Onesimus, and at the same time to his well-to-do master, Philemon.

Class Feature. Let the class consider briefly the Scripture passages given at the end of 2 Peter which show that grace stands connected with service. P. 1320.

Questions

1. Why is service essential to a complete Christian life?
2. Can you show how Joshua was true to his favorite word "serve"?
3. Can you give examples of Ruth serving?
4. What conditions of service called Esther to show courage?
5. What offices did Christ represent in service?
6. What lesson is drawn from the passage in the Song of Solomon?
7. What are the three conditions of the fruitful life?
8. What comes from our bearing "much fruit"?
9. In what two ways do the Spirit and Christ bestow gifts for service on Christians?
10. How can we know that our service is subject to Christ's will?

Program 6

FELLOWSHIP AND WORSHIP

Steps in David's Experience. In the restoration of David to full communion with God, after his great sin, as disclosed in the Fifty-first Psalm, the fifth item, "service," is followed by (6) worship, and (7) fellowship. P. 623. This may show how appropriately Program 5 on Service is followed by the present Program on Fellowship and Worship in our unfolding of personal divine life.

The Stage of Leviticus. If we look at the key-note or "order of the experience of God's people" represented by the opening books of the Bible we find that "Genesis is the book of origins—of the beginning of life, and of ruin through sin. Exodus is the book of redemption, the first need of a ruined race. Leviticus is the book of worship and communion, the proper exercise of the redeemed."[1] This is the stage represented in this Program; and as worship and communion bring fellowship among those who so worship, the Program is entitled "Fellowship and Worship." It includes both fellowship of believers and their fellowship with God.

Meaning of Peace-Offering. The whole work of Christ in relation to the believer's peace is here in type. He *made* peace, Col. 1. 20; *proclaimed* peace, Eph. 2. 17; and *is* our peace, Eph. 2. 14. In Christ God and the sinner meet in peace. This makes prominent the thought of *fellowship* with God through Christ. Hence the peace-offering is set forth as affording food for the priests (Lev. 7. 31–34). Observe that it is the breast (affections) and shoulders (strength) upon which we as priests (1 Pet. 2. 9) feed in fellowship with the Father. This it is which makes the peace-offering especially a *thank-offering* (Lev. 7. 11, 12). P. 128.

Revived Spirit After the Captivity. One of the touching scenes of fellowship and worship came when the foundations of the temple were laid by the remnant who returned with Ezra: "They set the priests in their apparel with trumpets, and the Levites the sons of Asaph with cymbals, to praise the Lord after the ordinance of David King of Israel. And they sang together by course. . . . And all the people shouted with a great shout. . . . But many . . . who were ancient men, that had seen the first house . . . wept with a loud voice; and many shouted aloud for joy" (Ezra 3. 10–12). This occasion, marked by weeping mingled with rejoicing, reveals more clearly than perhaps does any other record the depth of feeling on the part of individual Israelites formed by their associations with the temple.

Longing for the Sanctuary. The desire to share once more the privileges of the sanctuary along with fellow worshippers finds nowhere else in the Word such intense expression as in the Eighty-fourth Psalm. "My soul longeth, yea, even fainteth for the courts of the Lord. . . . A day in thy courts is better than a thousand" (Psa. 84. 2, 10).

New Aspects of the Sabbath. The Christian first day perpetuates in the dispensation of grace the principle that one seventh of the time is especially sacred, but in all other respects is in contrast with the sabbath. . . . The first day is one of voluntary worship and service. Pp. 1011, 1012.

Class Feature. Let the class carefully yet briefly weigh practical questions relating to "the Christian first day" and meetings for fellowship and worship.

Rending of the Veil. The veil which was rent was the veil which divided the holy place into which the priests entered from the holy of holies into which only the high priest might enter on the day of atonement. It

---

[1] From the summary of the Pentateuch, page 2.

signified that a "new and living way" was opened for all believers to Christ, and to the future purposes of God. P. 1189.

Living in Fellowship. To walk in the light is to live in fellowship with the Father and the Son. Sin interrupts, but confession restores that fellowship. Immediate confession keeps the fellowship unbroken. P. 1321.

Questions

1. In the seven steps giving David's line of restoration to divine communion in Psalm 51, what two steps follow "service"?
2. What stage is represented by Genesis?
3. What by Exodus?
4. What by Leviticus?
5. What bearing had the peace-offering on fellowship?
6. What occasion after the captivity gives insight into ancient fellowship and worship?
7. What Psalm reveals the Israelite's intense longing for the sanctuary?
8. How do we view the Christian first day as respects observance, assemblies, fellowship, and worship?
9. What was signified by the rending of the veil of the temple?
10. How does John in his first Epistle determine the conditions of fellowship?

Program 7

UNION WITH GOD AND FULNESS OF THE SPIRIT

The Goal. Personal divine life has its goal in complete union with God. While to some it might appear too high an ideal, yet very early in the history of the race we have the record that "Enoch walked with God" (Gen. 5. 24). Again, Abraham lived so intimately in communion with his Maker that he was called "the Friend of God" (Jas. 2. 23).

Not to be Denied. There are natures that will not be denied in their search for living contact with God. Jacob, imperfect at many points, cried as he wrestled with the angel: "I will not let thee go, except thou bless me" (Gen. 32. 26). Moses greatly desired to see "the glory of God" (Ex. 33. 18), probably not through curiosity, but because he craved to be like God in character.

Among the Prophets. When in introducing the First Book of Kings reference is made to "the mighty ministry of Elijah," p. 385, we recognize that it is possible to use such language respecting the prophet and his work because of his remarkable intimacy with his heavenly Source of strength. Doubtless we would say that Jeremiah had a more difficult mission to perform as a prophet than Elijah, because it had to be carried out through a long series of years in the face of intense opposition by both leaders and people. Elijah often had the people with him, but in only a small measure did Jeremiah. What, then, was the secret of his strength? It was the pledge and experience of God's presence with him. "I am with thee, saith the Lord, to deliver thee" (Jer. 1. 8, 19). Jeremiah lived and wrought in communion with God.

Among the Psalmists. Among the writers of the Psalms some of the choice spirits of ancient Israel became articulate. Through these hymns, prayers, and poems it is possible for us to know the exact inner life of many children of God several centuries before the advent of our Lord. No other such words ever rang more true to life. Therefore, we know that we look directly into the hearts of some of the men and women of the generations from David onward when we find such expressions as these: "Whom have I in heaven but thee? and there is none upon earth that I desire beside thee" (Psa. 73. 25). "My soul shall be satisfied as with marrow and fatness; and my mouth shall praise thee with joyful lips: when I remember thee upon my bed, and meditate on thee in the night watches" (Psa. 63. 5, 6). We have here the unmistakable note of those who are living in conscious and joyful communion with God.

Secret of Remnant. In the history of Israel a "remnant" may be discerned—a spiritual Israel within the national Israel. P. 1205. Unquestionably the one feature which united the remnant through the whole period of its existence was the members' spiritual knowledge of and nearness to God.

Abiding in Christ. To abide in Christ is, on the one hand, to have no known sin unjudged and unconfessed, no interest or phase of life into which He does not enter. On the other hand, the abiding one takes all burdens to Christ, and draws all wisdom, life, and strength from Him. P. 1137. There results the state revealed by Paul's words in Gal. 2. 20, "Not I, but Christ," made possible because of the believer's vital union to Christ, and wholly the fruit of the Spirit in those yielded to Him. P. 1247. The life of God which is in the believer is an unsevered part of the life which eternally was, and eternally is, in Christ Jesus—one life, in Him and in the believer—Vine and branches; Head and members. P. 1353.

Class Feature. Let the leader direct the discussion of the class upon personal and practical standards of attainment of divine union, after which may occur brief prayers.

Spirit Fillings. Every believer is born of the Spirit; indwelt by the Spirit, whose presence makes the believer's body a temple; and baptized by the Spirit, thus sealing him for God. The New Testament distinguishes between having the Spirit, in ways just noted, which is true of all believers, and being filled with the Spirit, which is the believer's privilege and duty. The divine order is—"One baptism, many fillings." P. 1149.

Questions

1. What was most marked about Enoch?
2. Why was a special title given to Abraham?
3. What experience in the life of Jacob caused him to be called Israel?
4. What great desire possessed Moses?
5. What may it have meant?
6. Why did Jeremiah need special assurance from God?
7. What expressions from Psalmists show joyful communion with God?
8. What experience was a bond uniting the members of the "remnant" through its history?
9. Can you explain what is involved in "abiding in Christ"?
10. How do you distinguish a believer as Spirit-baptized and Spirit-filled?

25 Review and Test Questions on Course VI
(For directions see Note on page 29)

1. Can you find out the personal factor in the Bible account of creation? P. 106.

2. What series of persons can you suggest in the Old Testament under patriarchs, judges, kings, prophets, by about two names for each? P. 106.

3. Why can we say that Christ is the pivotal Person? P. 106.

4. How would you prove that the Bible movement is more and more from outward to inward life? Pp. 106, 107.

5. Can you show that discipline—the forming of right habits—has a place in all young life? P. 108.

6. What part of Israel's course from Egypt to Canaan is viewed as helpful discipline? P. 108.

7. What are some of the means by which the chosen people were taught in early times? P. 108.

8. What books of the Old Testament may bear witness to a growing moral and religious knowledge? P. 110.

9. How do the terms "Enlightenment" and "Assurance" in some New Testament epistles show growing knowledge and guidance? P. 110.

10. Why does the Christian have a "full-knowledge" that outranks what human efforts can give? P. 111.

11. Why does danger of turning aside accompany all stages of spiritual growth? Pp. 112, 113.

12. Can you give examples of Hebrew rulers who took by-paths? P. 112.

13. What do you understand "legalism" means as a by-path which Christians might now enter? P. 113.

14. Why does David's penitential prayer in the fifty-first Psalm approach the gospel experience? P. 114.

15. Can we say that God in the material universe meets the tests of science; and in the case of prayer those of the divine family? P. 114.

16. What are some things taught by the Lord's Prayer? P. 114.

17. Can you show that Joshua's favorite word, "serve," reveals his spirit of service? P. 116.

18. Is Christ's desire for "much fruit" from His disciples a call to service? Pp. 116, 117.

19. For what end are spiritual gifts and offices bestowed on Christians by the Holy Spirit? P. 117.

20. What uses has the Christian first day of the week for fellowship and worship compared with the Jewish Sabbath? P. 118.

21. What meaning has the rending of the veil of the temple for the freedom of Christian fellowship and worship? Pp. 118, 119.

22. What effect has sin on our fellowship with God? P. 119.

23. What is the goal in the development of personal divine life? P. 120.

24. Can you give an expression out of the Psalms showing that the writer had conscious and joyful communion with God? P. 120.

25. What range of experience is covered by the expression "Abiding in Christ"? P. 120.

COURSE VII
MAIN BIBLE DOCTRINES

COURSE VII

MAIN BIBLE DOCTRINES

General View

ORDERLY SUCCESSION OF REVEALED TRUTH	
1. God in Creation and Redemption.	5. Repentance, Faith, and Conversion.
2. Man's Primal Estate and Fall.	6. Outreaching of Christian Ideals.
3. Sin in Essence and Effects.	7. The Church and the Kingdom of God.
4. Christ's Nature, Advent, and work.	8. Christ's Return, the Kingdom of Heaven, and the Future.

Natural Order of Doctrines. It will be found that any full survey of Bible doctrines, whether treated very simply or very elaborately, arranges itself in a regular or natural order. Design A, as seen below, shows a movement that is called a "circuit" of doctrines. This is its nature. It is a circuit or cycle, which begins with the outgoing of God in creation. If

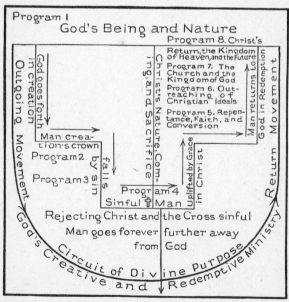

DESIGN A—CIRCUIT AND CONNECTIONS OF MAIN BIBLE DOCTRINES

we ask why God should have created the universe and man, we shall find, in Program 1, that He is the self-existent One who reveals Himself. It is the very nature of God as the God of love to find self-expression by calling into being creatures who can in sufficient measure understand Him and respond to His love. The fall intervenes and calls for redemption, but the movement passes through its circuit and in the end brings men back to God.

The Eight Programs. The substance of the eight Programs of this Course, as given opposite, showing their orderly succession and vital connections, is the demonstration or proof that we have in reality and in the Bible this cycle, swinging out from and returning to God. As we now take up successive features of Design A, we see that Program 1, starting with God's being and nature, follows His steps as He goes forth in creation, ending with man as creation's crown. Man's nature and his fall are covered in Program 2, and the movement goes to the lower level of sinful man, where Program 3 views sin in essence and effects. But God's purpose is not defeated, and in a second and greater outgoing movement He enters upon His ministry of redemption, and Program 4 shows the direct line descending from God to sinful man, in Christ's Advent and sacrificial offering, and lo, the cross is planted right beside sinful man. Some of the race reject Christ and the cross and go forever further away from God. But the others begin to be uplifted by grace in Christ, and presently repentance, faith, and conversion appear' in Program 5. A very important level is reached at conversion; but the believer is not to stop at this stage, valuable as it is; and Program 6 considers the outreaching of Christian ideals to the fullest possible for man and the world. In Program 7 we find we have attained the present stage of the professed church and the kingdom; and in Program 8, with Christ's second Advent, the millennium, or kingdom of heaven, and the eternal future, the circuit of doctrine is complete and man is brought back to God.

Doctrinal Circuit Disclosed in the Bible. The broad background of this doctrinal circuit pervades the Panoramic View at the front of the Bible, in such features as one God, progressive unfolding of truth, preparation for Christ, His manifestation, His work in the believer and in the church explained, and the consummation in closing judgments and heaven. This gives the movement as shown in the books of the Bible. Again, the Panoramic View takes the Human Story and sketches the creation of the earth and man, the early race record after the fall, the emergence and history of Israel as the people used to bring in redemption, the appearance of Christ the Messiah, his rejection, crucifixion, development of the church, completion of humanity's story, and final triumph of Christ. Thus we have passed again through the great doctrinal circuit. If we take Genesis for creation, sin, and fall, Exodus for redemption, Leviticus for access, restoration, and worship, Numbers for walk, and Joshua for final heavenly state, we see once more the outlines of the circuit. Each of the Gospels measurably gives it, and Paul, writing his most important Epistle and purposely treating doctrine, passes through the whole circuit very fully in Romans. It is therefore our task in this Course to make the best use of these sources and to present this cycle of Bible doctrines.

Program 1

GOD'S NATURE AND CHARACTER AND HIS CREATIVE AND REDEMPTIVE MINISTRY

God's Essential Being. The primary meaning of the name *Lord* (Jehovah) is "the self-existent One." Literally (as in Ex. 3. 14), "He *that* is who He is," therefore the eternal "I *am*." But *Havah*, from which Jehovah, or *Yahwe*, is formed, signifies also "to become," that is, to become known, thus pointing to a continuous and increasing self-revelation. Combining these meanings of *Havah*, we arrive at the meaning of the name Jehovah. He is "the self-existent One who reveals Himself." The name is, in itself, an advance upon the name "God" (*El, Elohim*), which suggests certain *attributes* of Deity, as strength, etc., rather than His essential *being.* P. 6.

Unity and Tri-unity. Israel was called to be a witness to the unity of God in the midst of universal idolatry. P. 19; Deut. 6. 4. The Supreme Being is One, but in some sense not fully revealed in the Old Testament, is a unity in plurality. This is shown by the plural name, Elohim, and by the use of the plural pronoun in the interrelation of Deity (Isa. 6. 8). That this plurality is really a Trinity is intimated in the three primary names of Deity, and in the threefold ascription, "Holy, holy, holy," of the seraphim. P. 983. At the baptism of Christ, for the first time the Trinity, foreshadowed in many ways in the Old Testament, is fully manifested. The Spirit descends upon the Son, and at the same moment the Father's voice is heard from heaven. P. 997. Father, Son, and Holy Spirit *is* the final name of the one true God. The conjunction in one name of the Three affirms *equality* and oneness of substance. P. 1044.

New Aspect in Creation. It is significant that the first appearance of the name Jehovah in Scripture follows the creation of man. It was God (*Elohim*) who said, "Let us make man in our image" (Gen. 1. 26); but when man, as in the second chapter of Genesis, is to fill the scene and become dominant over creation, it is the *Lord God* (*Jehovah Elohim*) who acts. This clearly indicates a special relation of Deity, in His Jehovah character to man, and all Scripture emphasizes this new aspect of God in His creative ministry. P. 6.

Distributor of the Earth. In accordance with the Gentile knowledge of God by His name "Most High," we read that "the Most High divided to the nations (that is, Gentiles) their inheritance, when he separated the sons of Adam," and "he set the bounds of the people according to the number of the children of Israel." World-wide adjustments are made as bearing upon God's purpose toward Israel. P. 23; Deut. 32. 8.

Class Feature. Let the class consider to what extent the mandates and other decisions concerning peoples and territory made after the World War had God in view as the Distributor of the earth.

Redemptive Ministry. Still more absolute is God's redemptive ministry, and Jehovah is distinctly the redemption name of Deity. When sin entered and redemption became necessary, it was Jehovah Elohim who sought the sinning ones and clothed them with "coats of skins," a beautiful type of righteousness provided by the *Lord* God through sacrifice. The first distinct *revelation* of Himself by his name Jehovah was in connection with the redemption of the covenant people out of Egypt (Ex. 3. 13–17). As Redeemer, emphasis is laid upon those attributes of Jehovah which the sin and salvation of man may bring into exercise. These are: (1) His holiness; (2) His hatred and judgment of sin; (3) His love for and redemption of sinners, but always righteously in the light of adequate

126

atonement, for salvation by Jehovah apart from sacrifice is unknown to Scripture. P. 6.

Questions

1. What is the primary meaning of the name Jehovah?
2. What is the full meaning?
3. How is God's tri-unity, or the Trinity, shown?
4. Where, in the Gospel account of Christ, is the Trinity fully manifested?
5. At what point in the Genesis account of creation does the Jehovah aspect of God appear?
6. How does God show Himself related to the earth as "The Most High"?
7. How did Jehovah indicate His redemptive ministry through sacrifice?
8. What is the first attribute of God as Redeemer?
9. What is the second attribute?
10. What is the third attribute?

Program 2

MAN'S PRIMAL ESTATE AND FALL

Steps of Approach to Man's Creation. Genesis is the book of origins, and we find in its opening chapter invaluable light on the origin of man. It supplants the often absurd and childish traditions from other sources with a revelation of orderly steps or stages. P. 2. Three creative acts of God are recorded in this opening chapter. The first is that of the heavens and the earth. This refers to the dateless past, and gives scope for all the geologic ages. The second creative act is of animal life, and the third is of human life. P. 3.

The Image of God. Man was made in the "image and likeness" of God. This "image" is found chiefly in man's tri-unity, and in his moral nature. Man is "spirit and soul and body." Pp. 5, 1270.

"Soul" in Man and Animal. "Soul" in itself implies self-conscious life, as distinguished from plants, which have unconscious life. In that sense animals also have "soul" (Gen. 1. 24); but the "soul" of man has a vaster content than "soul" as applied to beast life. P. 5.

Soul and Spirit Distinguished. That the human soul and spirit are not identical is proved by the facts that they are divisible (Heb. 4. 12), and that soul and spirit are sharply distinguished in the burial and resurrection of the body. It is sown a natural body (literally "soul-body"), it is raised a spiritual body (1 Cor. 15. 44). To assert, therefore, that there is no difference between soul and spirit is to assert that there is no difference between the mortal body and the resurrection body. P. 1270.

"Soul" in Scripture. As used in Scripture the soul is the seat of the *affections*, *desires*, and so of the *emotions*, and of the active *will*, the self. Thus Christ says, "My soul is exceeding sorrowful." The word translated "soul" in the Old Testament (*nephesh*) is the exact equivalent of the New Testament word for soul (Gr. *psuche*), and the use of "soul" in the Old Testament is identical with the use of that word in the New Testament. "Heart," in Scripture usage, is nearly synonymous with "soul." Because the natural man is, characteristically, the psychical man, "soul" is often used as synonymous with "individual" or "person," as when we read in Gen. 12. 5, that the patriarch took "the souls that they had gotten in Haran," in other words, the individuals or persons. Because man is "soul" he has self-consciousness, and can ask, "Why art thou cast down, O my soul?" (Psa. 42. 5). Pp. 5, 1270.

"Spirit" in Scripture. Again, in Scripture usage, we find that the spirit is that part of man which "knows" (1 Cor. 2. 11) his mind. The New Testament word for spirit (*pneuma*), like the Old Testament *ruach*, is translated "air," "breath," "wind," but predominantly "spirit," whether of God or of man. Because man is "spirit" he is capable of God-consciousness, and of communication with God. P. 1270.

Bodily Sphere. The body is separable from spirit and soul, and is susceptible of death; but is nevertheless an integral part of man, as the resurrection shows. It is the seat of the senses and of the fallen Adamic nature (Rom. 7. 23, 24). Through the bodily senses the spirit and soul have world-consciousness. P. 5.

Man's Fallen Condition. The first sin wrought the moral ruin of the race. The moral state of fallen man is described again and again in Scripture. This picture of mankind as fallen is given by the Psalmist: "The Lord looked down from heaven upon the children of men, to see if there were any that did understand, and seek God. They are all gone aside, they are all together become filthy; there is none that doeth good, no, not one" (Psa. 14. 2, 3). Christ confirms this view of man's natural condition when He says: "From within, out of the heart of men, proceed evil thoughts, adulteries, fornications, murder, thefts, covetousness, wickedness, deceit, lasciviousness, an evil eye, blasphemy, pride, foolishness" (Mk. 7. 21, 22). P. 1197.

Class Feature. Let there be a brief discussion of the present understanding of what has been known as man's total depravity.

Questions

1. What steps of approach are given to man's creation?
2. In what chiefly does the image of God in man consist?
3. How is the soul of man distinguished from what might be called "soul" in plant and animal?
4. What points show that the soul and spirit are distinct?
5. What manifestations of man come from the soul?
6. What powers of man may we assign to the spirit?
7. What things inhere in the body?
8. What caused the fall of man?
9. What are some of the expressions used by the Psalmist to show man's sinful state?
10. What are some of the terms used by Christ to indicate evil things proceeding from man's heart?

Program 3

SIN IN ORIGIN, NATURE, AND EFFECTS

Beginning of Sin. Most impressive among the sublime outbursts of Isaiah are these words: "How art thou fallen from heaven, O Lucifer, son of the morning! how art thou cut down to the ground, which didst weaken the nations. For thou hast said in thine heart, I will ascend into heaven, I will exalt my throne above the stars of God: I will sit also upon the mount of the congregation, . . . I will ascend above the heights of the clouds; I will be like the Most High. Yet thou shalt be brought down to hell, to the sides of the pit" (Isa. 14. 12–15). Lucifer, "day-star," can here be none other than Satan. This tremendous passage marks the beginning of sin in the universe. When the archangel Lucifer in an attitude of revolt against God Himself said, "I will," sin began. P. 726.

Satan in Serpent Form. When sin was about to invade this world through the temptation of our first parents by Satan, he appears to have gained possession of a serpent form. This creature, in its Edenic aspect, is not to be thought of as a writhing reptile. That is the effect of the curse (Gen. 3. 14). The serpent which lent itself to Satan may well have been the most beautiful as it was the most "subtle" of creatures less than man. Traces of that beauty remain despite the curse. P. 8.

Nature of Sin. The real nature of sin is shown in its several manifestations. Sin is: (1) *transgression*, an overstepping of the law, the divine boundary between good and evil; (2) *iniquity*, an act inherently wrong, whether expressly forbidden or not; (3) *error*, a departure from right; (4) *missing the mark*, a failure to meet the divine standard; (5) *trespass*, the intrusion of self-will into the sphere of divine authority; (6) *lawlessness*, spiritual anarchy; (7) *unbelief*, an insult to the divine veracity. P. 1194.

Facts Pertaining to Sin. 1. Sin originated with Satan; 2. it entered the world through Adam; 3. it was and is universal, Christ alone excepted; 4. it incurs the penalties of spiritual and physical death; 5. it has no remedy but in the sacrificial death of Christ availed of by faith. P. 1194.

Threefold Aspect. The realm of sin may be summarized under three aspects. If we view it, as we have above, as a nature, it is enmity toward God; if as an act, it is the violation of or want of obedience to the revealed will of God; if as a state it is absence of righteousness. P. 1194.

Physical Death an Effect of Sin. There are three steps in the demonstration that physical death is an effect of sin. 1. It is universal (Rom. 5. 12): all die—sinless infants, moral people, religious people, equally with the depraved. For a universal effect there must be a universal cause, namely, a state of universal sin. 2. This universal state must have had a cause: the consequence of Adam's sin was that "the many were made sinners" (Rom. 5. 19)—"by the offence of one judgment came upon all men unto condemnation" (Rom. 5. 18). 3. Personal sins are not meant here. From Adam to Moses death reigned (Rom. 5. 14), although there being no law, personal guilt was not imputed. Accordingly, from Gen. 4. 7 to Ex. 29. 14 the sin-offering is not once mentioned. Then, since physical death from Adam to Moses was not due to the sinful acts of those who die, it follows that it was due to a universal sinful *state* or nature, and that state is declared to be our inheritance from Adam. P. 1197.

Spiritual Death a Further Effect. Spiritual death, as an effect of sin, is the state of the natural or unregenerate man as still in his sins (Eph. 2. 1), alienated from the life of God, and destitute of the Spirit. P. 1251.

Class Feature. The class may canvass the question as to how far in the realm of nature we can trace the effect of Adam's sin when he "drew down into his ruin the old creation (Rom. 8. 19-22) of which he was lord and head." Pp. 1197, 1198.

Questions

1. How does the Bible appear to indicate that sin began in the universe?
2. What form did Satan assume in the first temptation?
3. Can you give several terms which express phases of sin, indicating the aspect which each brings out?
4. What is *transgression?*
5. What is *iniquity?*
6. What is *error?*
7. What is *trespass?*
8. How general is sin?
9. What are its penalties?
10. What is its remedy?

Program 4

CHRIST'S NATURE, ADVENT, AND WORK

General Proofs of Christ's Deity. The deity of Christ is declared in Scripture, the approach being made in the intimations and explicit predictions of the Old Testament. The theophanies, or manifestation of Deity in the form of angels and otherwise, prepare the way for the appearance of God in human form, and His ministry thus to man. We find that the Messiah is expressly declared to be the Son of God and God. His virgin birth is foretold as the means by which He becomes "Immanuel," God with us (Isa. 7. 14). Pp. 1144, 1145.

Christ's Own Assertions. Christ Himself affirmed His deity. He applied to Himself the term, "I AM." He asserted His identity with the Father. He exercised the divine prerogative of forgiving sin. He asserted omnipresence, omniscience, omnipotence, mastery over nature, and creative power. He received and approved human worship. P. 1145.

New Testament Writers. The New Testament writers ascribe to Christ: 1. divine titles, 2. divine perfections and attributes, 3. divine works. They teach that supreme worship should be paid to Him. Their establishing of His holiness and resurrection completes the proof of His deity. P. 1145.

Christ Seen by Luke. Luke relates those things concerning Jesus which demonstrate how entirely human He was. His genealogy is traced to Adam, and the most detailed account is given of His mother, and of His infancy and boyhood. But Luke is careful to guard the Deity and Kingship of Jesus. Luke is the Gospel of the human-divine One, as John is of the divine-human One. P. 1070.

Christ's Advent. In the third chapter of Genesis under the Adamic Covenant begins the line which includes the promises and prophecies concerning Christ which were fulfilled in His birth and works at His first advent. P. 9. When we read, in the seventh chapter of Isaiah: "Behold, a virgin shall conceive and bear a son, and shall call his name Immanuel," we may perceive that it was a continuing prophecy addressed to Mary in the annunciation of the angel Gabriel (Lev. 1. 35, 38). The passage in Isaiah adds: "Butter and honey shall he eat," thus indicating the plainness and simplicity of the life in which the young Immanuel should be brought up. P. 719.

Sacrificial Aspects of Christ's Work. The atonement of Christ, as interpreted by the Old Testament sacrificial types, has these necessary elements: 1. It is substitutionary—the offering takes the offerer's place in death. 2. The law is not evaded but honoured—every sacrificial death was an execution of the sentence of the law. 3. The sinlessness of Him who bore our sins is expressed in every animal sacrifice—it must be without blemish. 4. The effect of the atoning work of Christ is typified (1) in the promises, "it shall be forgiven him"; and (2) in the peace-offering, the expression of fellowship—the highest privilege of the saint. Pp. 148, 149. The value of the "life" is the measure of the value of the "blood." This gives the blood of Christ its inconceivable value. When it was shed the sinless God-man gave His life. It is not the blood in the veins of the sacrifice, but the blood *upon the altar* which is efficacious. The Scripture knows nothing of salvation by the imitation or influence of Christ's life, but only by that life yielded up on the cross. P. 150.

Complete New Testament View. As foreshadowed by the types and explained in the New Testament, the sacrifice of Christ is *penal; substitutional; voluntary; reconciling; propitiatory; efficacious;* and *revelatory.* P. 1300.

132

How Christ Propitiates. Christ so honoured the law by enduring its righteous sentence that God, who ever foresaw the cross, is vindicated in having "passed over" sins from Adam to Moses, and the sins of believers under the old covenant, and just in justifying sinners under the new covenant. There is no thought in propitiation of placating a vengeful God, but by doing right by His holy law and so making it possible for Him righteously to show mercy. P. 1195.

Class Feature. The class may well give the time for discussion to a consideration of the Sacrifice of Christ, as presented in the Summary on the preceding page.

Questions

1. What name or title and conditions of birth, as given in Isaiah 7. 14, indicate Christ's deity?
2. What did Christ claim when He said: "Before Abraham was, I am" (John 8. 58)?
3. How did Christ show mastery over nature?
4. When did He use creative power?
5. To whom does Luke trace the genealogy of Christ?
6. What is signified when the animal for sacrifice must be without blemish?
7. Why does Christ's blood have such great value?
8. Where must the blood be presented to have value?
9. Has God a vengeful feeling that needs to be placated?
10. What point then needs to be satisfied in order to justify those who have sinned?

Program 5

REPENTANCE, FAITH, AND CONVERSION

Passing a Spiritual Meridian. When a tourist makes the circuit of the globe, there comes a time when he passes the meridian most distant from the port where he embarked. Not always will he know when he passes the line or point marking one-half way round the world in any specific case. All we need to consider is that, when a tourist passes the half-way point, he is no longer going farther away from his home or starting-point, but he is verging toward home. So in the circuit of Bible doctrine, when we pass the point where Christ's sacrificial offering for mankind is complete, we are no longer moving outward from God but are verging back toward Him. It seems to the believer as he looks back that there is a longer or shorter stage where he is uplifted by grace in Christ, so that the goodness of God leads him to repentance.

Term in the Old Testament. In the Old Testament, repentance is the English word used to translate the Hebrew *nacham*, to be "eased" or "comforted." It occurs with both God and man. But while we have given the literal meaning of *nacham* it is evident that the Old Testament writers use it in the sense of *metanoia* in the New Testament—a change of mind. As in that part of Scripture, such a change of mind is often accompanied by contrition and self-judgment. P. 972.

Repentance in the New Testament. Repentance, being the translation of the Greek word *metanoia*, meaning "to have another mind" or "to change the mind," is used in the New Testament to indicate a change of mind in respect of sin, of God, and of self. Sorrow for sin, though it may "work" repentance, is not repentance. There must be reversal of course or of moral attitude. Saving faith includes or implies such a change of mind as constitutes true repentance. P. 1174.

Saving Faith. The essence of saving faith consists in receiving what God has revealed, and may be defined as that trust in the God of the Scriptures and in Jesus Christ whom He hath sent, which receives Him as Saviour and Lord, and impels to loving obedience and good works. More specifically for salvation, faith is personal trust, apart from meritorious works, in the Lord Jesus Christ, as delivered for our offences and raised again for our justification. P. 1302.

More General Uses of Faith. As used in prayer, faith is the confidence that we have in God, that "if we ask anything according to his will, he heareth us" (1 John 5. 14, 15). As used in reference to unseen things of which Scripture speaks, faith "gives substance" to them, so that we act upon the conviction of their reality (Heb. 11. 1-3). As a working principle in life, the uses of faith are illustrated throughout the course of this eleventh chapter of Hebrews. Pp. 1302, 1303.

Changes Accompanying Conversion. The individual remains the same and yet not the same in conversion. In the Lord the natural affections are sanctified and lifted to the level of the divine love. P. 1096. As a broad, general statement, conversion shows how partial, weak, and inadequate is law; but how marvelous, divine, and sufficient is grace. Law is connected with Moses and works; grace with Christ and faith. Law blesses the good; grace saves the bad. Law demands that blessings be earned; grace is a free gift. P. 1115. Then, conversion reveals its supernatural character because it calls for the new birth. Through conversion and regeneration the believer becomes a partaker of the divine nature and of the life of Christ Himself. Pp. 1117, 1118.

Adoption. Adoption (*huiothesia*, "placing as a son") is not so much a word of *relationship* as of *position*. The believer's relation to

134

God as a child results from the new birth, whereas adoption is the act of God whereby one already a child is, through redemption from the law, placed in the position of an adult son. The indwelling Spirit gives the realization of this in the believer's present experience; but the full manifestation of the believer's sonship awaits the resurrection change, and translation of the saints, which is called "the redemption of the body" (Rom. 8. 23). P. 1250.

Class Feature. Let the leader aim tactfully and tenderly to draw out the members as to whether they personally know conversion to be a supernatural experience.

Questions

1. At what point does the circuit of doctrine move no longer outward but verge back toward God?
2. What then prepares the prospective believer to take the first step toward repentance?
3. What is the literal meaning of *nacham*, the Old Testament word for repentance?
4. But with what meaning is it actually used, along with the New Testament word, *metanoia?*
5. Repentance is a change of mind in respect of what three things?
6. Can you give the essence of what we mean by saving faith?
7. How may you describe faith as used in prayer by Christian people?
8. What change is there in the natural affections in true conversion?
9. What does conversion show respecting law and grace?
10. How does conversion prove itself superior to natural character?

Program 6

OUTREACHING OF CHRISTIAN IDEALS

Exalted Christian Standards. The glorious standards and lofty ideals of the Christian faith form one of its greatest elements of power. These high objectives are not impracticable nor impossible in view of the purpose of the Father, the love of Christ irradiating from the cross, the depths and heights of redeeming grace, and the unmeasured energies of the Holy Spirit.

Maturity of Godliness. When, in the Sermon on the Mount, Christ says: "Be ye therefore perfect, even as your Father which is in heaven is perfect," the word implies full development, growth into maturity of godliness, not sinless perfection. And the Father's kindness, not His sinlessness, is the point in question. P. 1001.

"Sons" or "Brethren." Christ brought out by His redemption all who believe from the place of servants under the law into the place of sons, and therefore heirs, of God (Gal. 4. 7). He mediates by His blood the new covenant of assurance and grace in which all believers stand; and in this way He establishes the "law of Christ" with its precepts of higher exaltation made possible by the indwelling Spirit. P. 1000. Thus, under the new covenant of grace the principle of obedience to the divine will is inwrought. P. 1245. As John's Gospel puts it, the progressive intimacy is: servants, John 13. 13; friends, John 15. 15; brethren, John 20. 17. P. 1137.

Law of Love and Liberty. The new "law of Christ" is the divine love, as wrought into the renewed heart by the Holy Spirit, and outflowing in the energy of the Spirit, unforced and spontaneous, toward the objects of the divine love. It is, therefore, the "law of liberty." P. 1326.

Christian Character. Christian character is not mere moral or legal correctness, but the possession and manifestation of nine graces: love, joy, peace (character as in inward state); longsuffering, gentleness, goodness (character in expression toward man); faith, meekness, temperance (character in expression toward God). This character is possible because of the believer's vital union to Christ. P. 1247.

Supremacy of Love. Gifts are good but only if ministered in love. Benevolence is good but not apart from love. Love is better than our present incomplete knowledge, and greater than even faith and hope. P. 1223.

"The Heavenlies." "The heavenlies" may be defined as the sphere of the believer's spiritual experience as identified with Christ in nature, life, relationships, service, suffering, inheritance, and future glory in the kingdom. P. 1249.

Separation. Separation in Scripture is twofold: "from" whatever is contrary to the mind of God; and "unto" God Himself. Separation is not from contact with evil in the world or the church, but from complicity with and conformity to it. P. 1234.

Natural, Spiritual, and Carnal. Paul divides men into three classes: first, *psuchikos*, or "natural," that is, the Adamic man, unrenewed through the new birth; then, we see that man, though a Christian, may be *sarkikos*, "carnal" or "fleshly," the renewed man who, walking "after the flesh," remains a babe. He is able to comprehend only the simplest Scripture truth that is likened to "milk" instead of "meat." Lastly, there is man as *pneumatikos*, or "spiritual," the renewed man as Spirit-filled and walking in the Spirit in full communion with God. P. 1213.

Priesthood of Believers. In the dispensation of grace, all believers are unconditionally constituted a "kingdom of priests." The chief privilege of a priest is access to God. When Christ died, the veil, type of Christ's human body, was rent, so that now the believer-priests, equally with Christ the High Priest, have access to God in the holiest. In the exercise of his office the New Testament believer-priest is a *sacrificer* who offers a threefold sacrifice: 1. his own living body; 2. praise to God, "the fruit of the lips that make mention of His name;" 3. his substance. He is also an *intercessor.* Pp. 1313, 1314.

The Believer Justified and Sanctified. Justification and sanctification are Scripturally viewed, first, as position or standing. "Christian position in grace is the result of the work of Christ, and is fully entered the moment that Christ is received by faith." P. 1211. So, justification is, first, the judicial act of God whereby He justly declares righteous one who believes on Jesus. As actual experience it marks the believer's life when, through the indwelling Spirit, the righteousness of the law is fulfilled in him. P. 1245. Likewise for sanctification, first, in position, believers are eternally set apart for God by redemption, "through the offering of the body of Jesus Christ once" (Heb. 10. 9. 10). Positionally, therefore, believers are "saints" and "holy" from the moment of believing. Second, in experience, the believer is being sanctified by the work of the Holy Spirit through the Scriptures. Third, in consummation, the believer's complete sanctification awaits the appearing of the Lord. P. 1353.

Class Feature. First, let the members of the class intimately and personally consider how fully these great Christian ideals have taken possession of their lives; and, second, let there be prayer for their more general embodiment in believers.

Questions

1. Why can we claim that the highest Christian standards and ideals are not impracticable nor impossible?

2. In what sense are we asked to be perfect as our Father in heaven is perfect?

3. By what means are we changed from the status of "servants" to that of "sons" or "brethren"?

4. Is it spiritually possible to unite law and liberty?

5. What three graces express character as an inward state?

6. What three express character toward men?

7. What three express character toward God?

8. What does Paul mean by the terms the natural, the carnal, and the spiritual man?

9. What threefold sacrifice can the believer-priest offer?

10. Can you show how justification and sanctification each have one meaning as relates to position, and another as relates to experience?

Program 7

THE CHURCH AND THE KINGDOM OF GOD

Literal Meaning of Term, Church. The Greek word, *ecclesia*, means an assembly of called-out ones, and in its literal meaning it implies no more, as the Israelites, called out of Egypt and assembled in the wilderness, are simply termed "the church in the wilderness" (Acts 7. 38). P. 1158.

Divine Purpose Shown. James, at the first council at Jerusalem, stated that God through Peter had visited the Gentiles "to take out of them a people for his name" (Acts 15. 14). He thus indicates that Peter's ministry in the house of Cornelius fulfilled God's purpose to call out from among the Gentiles those who, joined with the Jewish converts previously gathered, should begin the church for this age. Dispensationally this becomes the most important passage in the New Testament. P. 1169.

The Method Disclosed. The taking out from among the Gentiles of a people devoted in a special and spiritual manner to the name of God is the distinctive work of the church-age in which we are living. The movement has been in progress since Pentecost and the sermon to Cornelius and his company. The Gospel has never anywhere converted all, but everywhere has called out some. Pp. 1169, 1170. The blindness or unbelief of Israel during this period provides the Gentile opportunity, p. 1204, and the "remnant" during this era are the believing Jews. Thus, the "fulness of the Gentiles" (Rom. 11. 25) points to the purpose of God to form the church chiefly of Gentiles in this age. Pp. 1205, 1206.

Great Service of Paul. The sixteenth chapter of Matthew contains Christ's announcement of His purpose to build His church; but wholly without explanation as to how, when, or of what materials, that church should be built, or what should be its position, relationship, privileges, or duties. All this constitutes precisely the scope of the Epistles of Paul. They develop the doctrine of the church. In his letters to seven churches; namely, in Rome, Corinth, Galatia, Ephesus, Philippi, Colosse, and Thessalonica, the church, the "mystery which from the beginning of the world hath been hid in God" (Eph. 3. 9), is fully revealed, and she is fully instructed as to her unique place in the counsels and purposes of God. P. 1189.

The Church Christ's Body. Through Paul alone we know that the church is not an organization, but an organism, the body of Christ; instinct with His life, and heavenly in calling, promise, and destiny. Every believer is a member of Christ's body and is given a spiritual enablement for specific service through the Holy Spirit acting in free sovereignty. The gifts are diverse, but all are equally honourable because bestowed by the same Spirit, administered by the same Lord, and energized by the same God. These gifts must be governed by love, and the gift of prophecy must subject itself to order. Pp. 1222–1225.

The Church Christ's Bride. Again, the symbolism changes in Ephesians, and the church follows the type of Eve as the bride of the first man. In His love-work Christ has redeemed and is sanctifying the church, and He will present the church to Himself in flawless perfection, "one pearl of great price." Pp. 1254, 1255. At the close of Revelation the church appears as the Lamb's wife—the "heavenly Jerusalem." P. 1348.

The True and the Professing Church. The true church is composed of the whole number of regenerate persons from Pentecost to the first resurrection. P. 1304. But the visible church is that visible body of professed believers, existing under many names and divisions based upon differences in doctrine or in government. Within, for the most part, this historical church exists the true church, like the believing Remnant within Israel. The predicted future of the visible or professing church is apostasy; but of the true church glory. P. 1276.

The Kingdom of God. Of kindred nature to the true church, the kingdom of God is universal, including all moral intelligences willingly subject to the will of God, whether angels, the church, or saints of past or future dispensations. P. 1003.

Class Feature. Let the class inspect and discuss Design F of Course IV, on page 83 of these Courses, especially Division II as bearing on the Church-age; and follow with like use of Design B on page 141, stressing the "Opening Stages" or the "Church-age."

Questions

1. What is the literal meaning of the Greek word *ecclesia?*
2. What did James say was God's purpose in Peter's visit to the house of Cornelius?
3. Who chiefly compose the church in this age?
4. Who compose the Jewish remnant?
5. Where does Christ speak of His purpose to build His church?
6. Through whom was His manner of building it to be revealed?
7. Can you name the seven churches according to their cities or province, whose letters from Paul mean most for the doctrine of the church?
8. Under what two symbols or figures is the church presented?
9. Can you define or describe the true and the professing church?
10. Who are included in the Kingdom of God?

Program 8

CHRIST'S RETURN, THE KINGDOM OF HEAVEN, AND THE FUTURE

Climacteric Closing. It is evident, from the title of this Program and from the crowded series of great events entered in the period marked "Closing Stages—Kingdom-age," in Design B, that a climacteric closing is at hand.

The Two Advents. A tremendous summary of time from the opening of the Christian era to the end of the world is furnished by the two advents. These two periods, differing profoundly in the attitude and office of Christ in each, color the utterances of several of the prophets. We select the passage, Isaiah 61. 1, 2. Observe that Jesus suspended the reading of this passage in the synagogue at Nazareth (Luke 4. 16–21) at the comma in the middle of Isaiah 61. 2. The first advent, therefore, opened the day of grace, "the acceptable year of Jehovah," but does not fulfil the day of *vengeance* indicated in the clause which follows the comma. That will be taken up when the Messiah returns. P. 766.

The Resurrection of the Righteous. This event, called the "first resurrection" (Rev. 20. 5, 6), is placed in Design B as the great opening step connected with Christ's second advent. The bodies of all those who are Christ's own are raised and joined with the soul or spiritual nature. Paul describes this as being "caught up to meet the Lord in the air" (1 Thess. 4. 17). P. 1228. In anticipation of this we see the departure from heaven of Christ and the saints and angels. P. 1348.

The Great Tribulation, the Beast, and Armageddon. Shortly before Christ's return, or for about three and a half years, there is to be a period of unexampled trouble centering in Jerusalem and the Holy Land, called the great tribulation. P. 1337. This is due to the "beast" or evil leader (Rev. 14. 1–10) known as the "little horn" (Dan. 7. 8) or "man of sin" (2 Thess. 2. 3) directing the ten Gentile kingdoms of that time against God and the kingdom of good, especially the believing Jewish remnant. For, during the great tribulation a remnant out of all Israel will turn to Jesus as Messiah, and will become His witnesses after the removal of the church. Pp. 918, 919, 1205, 1337, 1349. Armageddon (the ancient hill and valley of Megiddo, west of the Jordan in the plain of Jezreel) is the appointed place for the beginning of the great battle in which the Lord at His coming in glory will deliver the Jewish remnant besieged by the Gentile world-powers under the Beast. Pp. 1348, 1349.

Christ's Return, or The Second Advent. At what precise point the Return, or Second Advent, of Christ should be placed among the many events that crowd this period may not at first be clear. Its entry is made in Design B at the point that seems most appropriate. The first resurrection has already occurred. As Paul puts it, "in a moment, in the twinkling of an eye," the righteous dead have been raised and the living believers have been "changed" or translated from the earthly to the immortal state, and have assembled with Christ. Pp. 1227, 1228, 1269. There has been the interval when the saved Jewish representatives have become missionary evangelists, and have experienced the period of great tribulation. Then Christ appears in power and glory. P. 1337.

The Day of Jehovah. The reach of this phase in the closing stages of time is shown in Design B. It begins with the return of the Lord in glory and ends in the purgation of the heavens and the earth by fire. P. 1349.

The Kingdom of Heaven, or the Kingdom-age. The phrase, kingdom of heaven, is peculiar to Matthew and is derived from Daniel. In its prophetic aspect it is the kingdom to be set up after the return of the

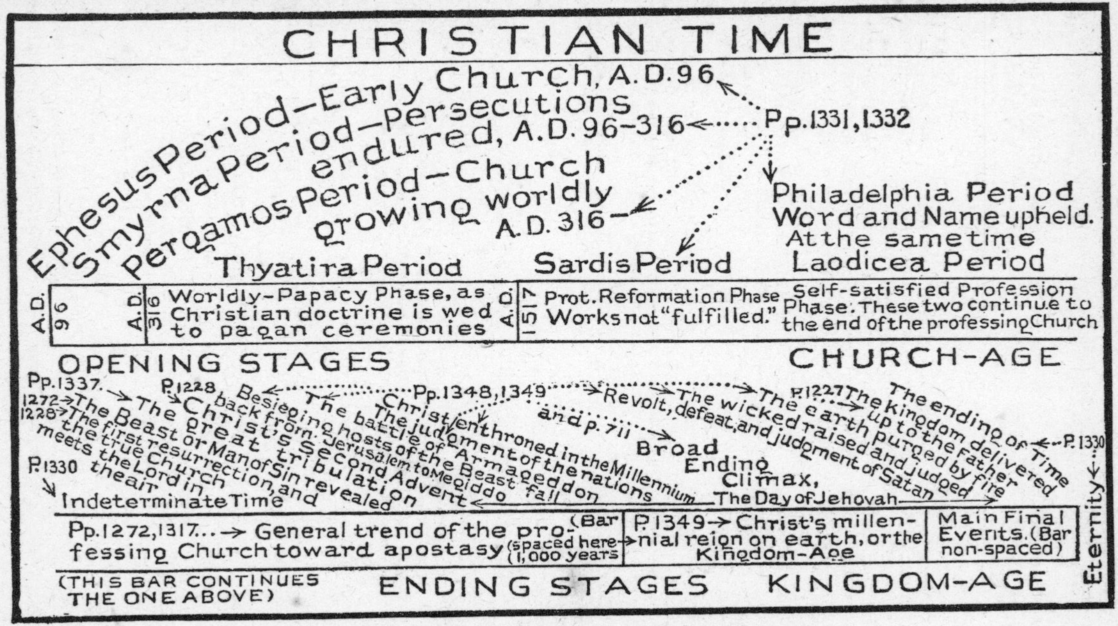

CHRISTIAN TIME

Ephesus Period — Early Church, A.D. 96

Smyrna Period — persecutions endured, A.D. 96-316

Pergamos Period — Church growing, worldly, A.D. 316

Pp. 1331, 1332

Philadelphia Period — Word and Name upheld.
At the same time
Laodicea Period — Self-satisfied Profession

Prot. Reformation Phase — "Works not 'fulfilled.'" These two continue to the end of the professing Church

CHURCH-AGE

Thyatira Period
Sardis Period

d | Worldly-Papacy Phase, as
A | Christian doctrine is wed
D | to pagan ceremonies

A.D. 96

OPENING STAGES

Pp. 1337.
1272→ The Christ back from heaven.
1228→ The Beast out of the great tribulation—
meets the first resurrection and
P. 1330 the true resurrection of
the Lord Jesus Christ, and
Indeterminate Time

P. 1228 Besieging the
Christ, the
judgment enthroned
hosts of. Armageddon
Jerusalem Beast
Man of Sin revealed and
air in tribulation and
revealed in Time

Pp. 1348, 1349.
→ Revolt, defeat, and p. 711

→ The wicked earth
and judgment of
the Armaments of the Millennium
delivered to Satan judged
Armageddon
The Day of Jehovah

P. 1227 The ending of
The kingdom up to the
earth raised at the
fire

Broad
Ending
Climax,

→ P. 1330

Eternity →

Main Final
Events. (Bar non-spaced)

P. 1349 → Christ's millennial reign on earth, or the
Kingdom-Age

ENDING STAGES   KINGDOM-AGE

Pp. 1272, 1317... → General trend of the professing Church toward apostasy

(Bar)
(spaced here)
(1,000 years)

(THIS BAR CONTINUES
THE ONE ABOVE)

DESIGN B—OPENING AND ENDING STAGES OF CHRISTIAN TIME

King in glory. P. 996. When Christ returns, the Dispensation of grace ceases and the Dispensation of the Kingdom begins. Thenceforward till the end of time the Kingdom of Heaven constitutes the Kingdom-age. Pp. 1227, 1250, 1341.

The Millennium. After the opening of the Kingdom-age a few events may precede the period known as the Millennium, and a few events may supplement that period; but, for the most part, the Dispensation of the Kingdom, the Kingdom-age, and the Millennium denote one and the same period. With Satan removed from the scene, while the enormous majority of earth's inhabitants will be saved, it is impossible to conceive to what heights of spiritual, intellectual, and physical perfection humanity will attain in this, its coming age of righteousness and peace. P. 977. Christ uses for this state of the world the profound term *palingenesia*, re-creation.—the re-creation of the social order and renewal of the earth. 1026. In the use of His designation "Son of Man," Christ's thought leaps forward to the time of His coming not to Israel only but to the race. 1006.

The Future. At the close of the millennium there are the revolt, defeat, and judgment of Satan; the wicked are raised and judged; the earth is purged by fire, p. 1349; and the kingdom is delivered up to the Father. P. 1227. Then comes the ending of time and the beginning of eternity. P. 1330. The eternal throne is that "of God, and of the Lamb" (Rev. 22. 1). P. 1227. The New Covenant rests upon the sacrifice of Christ, and secures the eternal blessedness of all who believe. P. 1298. And Christ's intercessory petition will be answered, that believers will be with Him in heaven to behold and share His glory. P. 1139.

Class Feature. Let the leader briefly touch upon the mountain-summits of truth in the Course, and offer prayer that all may in heaven behold and share Christ's glory.

Questions

1. How did Christ mark the two advents when he read Isaiah 61. 2 at Nazareth?
2. Where, in the period of Christ's return, do we place the resurrection of the righteous?
3. How long is the great tribulation, and who causes it?
4. Who constitutes those against whom the "man of sin" makes war?
5. Whence comes the name "Armageddon"?
6. What gives the battle significance?
7. Can you give about the extent of the day of Jehovah?
8. Will you explain the Kingdom of Heaven and the Kingdom-age?
9. How is the millennium related to the Kingdom-age?
10. Can you outline the events following the millennium and given under the heading "the Future"?

25 Review and Test Questions on Course VII
(For directions see Note on page 29)

1. Can you show that the unfolding of Christian doctrine forms a circuit, out from and back to God? Pp. 124, 125.
2. Does God in His nature tend to reveal Himself? P. 126.
3. What constitutes the unity and the tri-unity or Trinity of God? P. 126.
4. How does God in His redemptive ministry more fully reveal Himself? Pp. 126, 127.
5. What makes up the tri-unity or three parts of man's nature? P. 128.
6. Which part of man makes him self-conscious, and which God-conscious? P. 128.

7. What proves that man has sinned or fallen from his first estate? Pp. 128, 129.

8. Does the Bible give any account of the origin of sin in the universe? P. 130.

9. What may we regard as the real nature of sin? P. 130.

10. What are the effects of sin? P. 130.

11. Can you give some proofs of Christ's deity? P. 132.

12. Which of the Gospel writers brings out most clearly the humanity of Christ? P. 132.

13. In what consists the value of Christ's sacrifice? P. 132.

14. What is the thing that counts in repentance? P. 134.

15. Wherein is the essence of saving faith? P. 134.

16. Can you give some features of conversion? P. 134.

17. What are some of the graces that enter into Christian character? P. 136.

18. How do you prove the supremacy of love? P. 136.

19. How is a believer justified or sanctified as respects position or standing, and then as respects experience? P. 137.

20. What is the root-idea in the Bible term, "church"? P. 138.

21. Can you name some of the Epistles in which Paul explains the church? P. 138.

22. The church is often called Christ's "body." Can you give another term like this, as relates to Christ? P. 136.

23. How would you state Christ's return? P. 140.

24. Can you give some factors of the millennium? P. 142.

25. What things belong to the future, beyond the millennium? P. 142

50 Review and Test Questions on A Year's Bible Course

(For directions in general see Note on page 29. But note additionally that each question correctly answered on the entire book counts 2 in an examination test, and that 30 correctly answered, giving a mark of 60, may pass a person. Page numbers following these questions are those of the text-book.)

1. Why are there seven courses making up the full course? P. 7.

2. What is meant by the courses being called "balanced and two-hemisphered"? P. 8.

3. What is the goal or purpose of the entire course? P. 10.

4. Why is obedience so strongly emphasized in Genesis? P. 15.

5. Why is a sense of God's favour a leading theme in the Psalms? P. 16.

6. Why did the "Immanuel" prophecy in Isaiah mean much? P. 18.

7. How did Christ place sin in the motive, in His great sermon as given in Matthew? P. 20.

8. Can you give any words from the Gospel of John making Christ God? P. 23.

9. Can you give some features in Acts which outline Paul's work? Pp. 24, 25.

10. Why can it be said that Romans is the chief Epistle on doctrines? P. 26.

11. Can you cite words used in Hebrews to show that it deals especially with type or similitude? P. 28.

12. What evidence can you give that our first parents started in a state of innocence in Eden? P. 34.

13. What record shows that conscience became a working force with Adam and Eve? P. 36.

14. Why is human government a necessity in any organized society of mankind? P. 38.

15. Can you explain why a divine promise is a proper beginning of religion? Pp. 40, 41.

16. Why is law not a final solution of the religious needs of man? P. 42.

143

17. Why is grace an even larger religious word than promise? P. 44.

18. Can you show that the millennial kingdom of Christ on earth will solve many problems? Pp. 46, 47.

19. Why is the Pentateuch rich in types? P. 52.

20. Why were gold and acacia wood combined in the tabernacle and its furniture beautifully typical? P. 54.

21. Can you unfold the symbolism of fire as a type? P. 56.

22. Can you develop the symbols of cross and crown, as respects both Christ and the believer? P. 58.

23. How can we use the term "mysteries" and not make these parts of the Bible seem "mysterious"? P. 60.

24. Why did Christ give just seven parables of the Kingdom? Pp. 62, 63.

25. Why are all the Bible books largely veiled or cryptic to unbelievers? Pp. 64, 65.

26. In what sense is Christ in the Old Testament? Pp. 70–75.

27. What is the great purpose of the Gospels in their presentation of Christ? Pp. 76, 77, and Design D.

28. Who is the author of Acts, and how is it connected with a former book of his? P. 78.

29. What are two divisions of the Epistles, and how is Christ uplifted in each? P. 80.

30. How is the book of Revelation a consummation of Christ's mission? P. 82.

31. Of Elijah and Elisha, which represents teaching and which action? P. 88.

32. In which kingdom did Obadiah and Joel do their work? P. 90.

33. Which kingdom received the ministry of Amos and Hosea? Pp. 92, 93.

34. To what kingdom was Jonah sent? P. 94.

35. Can you give the contrasted environment of Isaiah and Micah? P. 96.

36. In what city was the chief service of Zephaniah, Habakkuk, and Jeremiah? Pp. 98, 99.

37. Can you give the somewhat neighboring locations of Daniel and Ezekiel? Pp. 100, 101.

38. In what province did Haggai, Zechariah, and Malachi minister? Pp. 102, 103.

39. What are the best lines of help that can be given the beginning Christian? Pp. 108–112.

40. What two invaluable habits or exercises belong in all parts of a Christian life? Pp. 114–117.

41. Can you touch some points in the history of fellowship and worship? Pp. 118, 119.

42. What are some inspiring examples and standards for the personal life? Pp. 120, 121.

43. With whom must the Bible and all doctrine begin? P. 126.

44. What offspring of God comes next in a survey of doctrine? P. 128.

45. What alien force enters and separates man from his Creator, God? P. 130.

46. What divine representative comes to counteract the effects of sin? P. 132.

47. How does the return of man to God begin? P. 134.

48. What are the highest earthly reaches of man toward God? Pp. 136, 137.

49. What are the highest ideals of organized Christianity? Pp. 138, 139.

50. What are the great transition stages to be carried through by Christ chiefly on earth? Pp. 140–142.

SUPPLEMENT

CONTAINING ANSWERS TO THE 745 QUESTIONS IN A
YEAR'S BIBLE COURSE

NOTE.—S. R. B. followed by a numeral means the given page of the
Scofield Reference Bible; T. B. followed by a numeral means the given
page of this Text Book.

Answers to Questions on Page 15 of Text Book

1. I. Creation. II. The Fall and Redemption. III. The Diverse
Seeds. IV. The Flood to Babel. V. From the call of Abram to the death
of Joseph. S. R. B. 3.

2. "The self-existent One who reveals Himself." Distinctly the
redemption name of Deity. S. R. B. 6.

3. Jehovah Elohim indicates a special relation of Deity, in His
Jehovah character, to man. S. R. B. 6.

4. Enoch (Gen. 5. 2); Noah (Gen. 6. 9). S. R. B. 13.

5. The marriage of the Cainites with the Sethites, and the building
of the tower of Babel. T. B. 14.

6. The flood and the confusion of tongues. T. B. 14.

7. A chosen race. T. B. 14; S. R. B. 19.

8. Faith, obedience, detachment from the world, and intimacy with
God.

9. A cripple in his own strength! "Jacob's thigh was out of joint."
A surrendered man. "He wept and made supplication unto him." (Hos.
12. 4).

10. Courageous utterance of truth, quiet trust under bitter trials,
victory over sudden temptation, efficient in high office, recognizing God's
providences, eminent in forgiveness of his brethren and in family affection.

Answers to Questions on Page 17 of Text Book

1. A sense of sin and appropriating faith.

2. At least eight leading terms for the Bible in Psalm 119: law,
word, testimonies, commandments, statutes, ordinances, precepts, judgments.

3. "Delighteth in the law of the Lord," "backbiteth not with his
tongue," "worketh righteousness." (Psa. 1. 2; 15. 2, 3).

4. Panting of the hart after the water brooks (Psa. 42. 1).

5. The feast of unleavened bread, the feast of firstfruits, and the
feast of ingathering (Ex. 23. 14–17).

6. "Rest in the Lord" (Psa. 37. 7).

7. "He shall cover thee with his feathers, . . . his truth shall be thy
shield and buckler. There shall no evil befall thee." "I will deliver him,
and honour him" (Psa. 91. 4, 10, 15).

"They are not in trouble as other men." "Their eyes stand out
with fatness: they have more than heart could wish." "Their tongue
walketh through the earth." "They increase in riches" (Psa. 73. 5, 7,
9, 12).

9. Psa. 107. 8, 15, 21, 31.

10. Trumpet, psaltery, harp, timbrel, cymbals (Psa. 150. 3–5).

Answers to Questions on Page 19 of Text Book

1. He has the more comprehensive testimony and is distinctively
the prophet of redemption. S. R. B. 713.

2. Early but strong manhood, loftiness of spirit, wideness of prophetic vision, statesmanship, devotion to God and nation.

3. Luxury, especially among women (Isa. 3. 16–23), injustice and monopoly (Isa. 3. 14, 15; 5. 7), superstition and astrology (Isa. 47. 13).

4. It is the collapse of self! Similar to the experience of Joshua, Job, Ezekiel, Daniel, and John, as indicated at head of chapter (Isa. 6).

5. Assyria (Isa. 8. 7, 8).
6. Uzziah, Jotham, Ahaz, Hezekiah (Isa. 1. 1).
7. Hezekiah (Isa. 35. 1).
8. Babylonia (Isa. 47. 1), Persia (Isa. 45. 1).
9. Persia.
10. Isaiah 53d chapter.

Answers to Questions on Page 21 of Text Book

1. The Davidic Covenant and the Abrahamic Covenant.
2. Six. S. R. B. 994.
3. The kingdom of heaven is the Messianic earth rule of Jesus Christ, the Son of David. S. R. B. 996.
4. The kingdom of God is universal, including all moral intelligences willingly subject to the will of God. S. R. B. 1003.
5. Christ's baptism may be viewed as the washing preceding the anointing with the Holy Spirit, and also as His taking His place with the believing remnant. S. R. B. 997.
6. Satan's object was to induce Christ to act from Himself, in independency of His Father. S. R. B. 997.
7. To declare the *principles* of the kingdom. S. R. B. 999.
8. Matt. 11. 20–27; 27. 31–37. S. R. B. 1011.
9. The hiding of the Father's face. S. R. B. 1038.
10. God freely gives to him eternal life, accounts to him a perfect righteousness; and accords to him a perfect position. S. R. B. 1044.

Answers to Questions on Page 23 of Text Book

1. *Logos*, as a Greek term, means, (1) a thought or concept; (2) the expression or utterance of that thought. S. R. B. 1114.
2. The Person, and "thought" of Deity. S. R. B. 1114.
3. Not a reformation of the old nature, but a creative act of the Holy Spirit. S. R. B. 1117, 1118.
4. The centurion (Matt. 8. 5–13), and the Greeks (John 12. 20, 21).
5. The blood of Christ answers forever to all the law could say as to the believer's *guilt*, but he needs constant cleansing from the *defilement* of sin. S. R. B. 1134.
6. "One called alongside to help," S. R. B. 1136.
7. "Comforter" (John 14. 16, etc.), "Advocate" (1 John 2. 4). S. R. B. 1136.
8. Christ is the Believer's Paraclete with the Father when he sins; the Holy Spirit the believer's indwelling Paraclete to help his ignorance and infirmity, and to make intercession. S. R. B. 1136.
9. As God. T. B. 23; S. R. B. 990.
10. He applied to Himself the Jehovistic I AM (John 8. 24, 56–58; 10. 33; 18. 4–6). He asserted His identity with the Father (John 10. 30). He asserted omnipresence (Mt. 18. 20). S. R. B. 1145.

Answers to Questions on Page 25 of Text Book

1. Peter and Paul. S. R. B. 1147.
2. Jews. S. R. B. 1147.
3. Jerusalem. S. R. B. 1147.
4. To the Jews at Pentecost. S. R. B. 1147.
5. To the Gentiles in the house of Cornelius. S. R. B. 1147.
6. Antioch. S. R. B. 1147.
7. Gentiles. S. R. B. 1147.
8. His three missionary journeys; his arrest in Jerusalem and in

prison ment for two years at Cæsarea; and his trials, appeal to Cæsar, voyage to Rome, and ministry there though a prisoner. T. B. 25.

9. He returned to Jerusalem, subsequent to his conversion and conferred with Peter and James, the leaders there (Acts 9. 27; Gal. 1. 18, 19). He reported the work among Gentiles that marked his first missionary journey to the council at Jerusalem, and co-operated in reporting its decrees, which tended to harmonize Jewish and Gentile Christians (Acts 15. 12, 25–32). He collected and brought relief funds from the outside churches to the church at Jerusalem to help its more needy members (Acts 11 29, 30; Rom. 15. 25–28).

10. Probably two Roman imprisonments. S. R. B. 1188.

Answers to Questions on Page 27 of Text Book

1. Thirteen. T. B. 26.
2. Romans. T. B. 26.
3. The spiritual body of Christ. S. R. B. 1189.
4. Sin and guilt, salvation, redemption, grace, faith, forgiveness, justification. S. R. B. 1192–1195.
5. In a state of sin and guilt. S. R. B. 1191.
6. Sin is *transgression, trespass, lawlessness.* S. R. B. 1194.
7. The judicial act of God whereby He justly declares righteous one who believes on Jesus Christ. S. R. B. 1195.
8. Being saved in the sense of entire conformity to Christ. S. R. B. 1192.
9. For man, Christ Himself, who fully met in our stead and behalf every demand of the law. S. R. B. 1194. For God, His consistency with His own law and holiness in freely justifying a sinner who believes in Christ. S. R. B. 1195.
10. By the power of the Holy Spirit. T. B. 27.

Answers to Questions on Page 29 of Text Book

1. It has been in controversy from the earliest times. S. R. B. 1291.
2. Before the destruction of the Temple, A. D. 70. S. R. B. 1291.
3. To confirm Jewish Christians by showing that Judaism had come to an end through the fulfilment by Christ of the whole purpose of the law; and to keep Jewish professed believers from either lapsing back into Judaism or pausing short of true faith in Jesus Christ. S. R. B. 1291.
4. It contrasts the types of the old or Mosaic Covenant with the eternal or unchangeable type or reality presented in Christ and the New Covenant, showing that at every point the latter is superior. S. R. B. 1297.
5. "Better."
6. Spiritual beings, executives of God's will, therefore some are "sent forth to minister to them who shall be heirs of salvation." S. R. B. 1292.
7. A perfect rest of mercy and grace, through the Son of God. S. R. B. 1294.
8. After the order of Melchisedec as to *person, appointment,* and *duration,* but after the order of Aaron in His *work.* S. R. B. 1295.
9. They were types expressing the guilt and need of the offerer in reference to God, and all pointing to Christ. S. R. B. 1300.
10. According to the example of Jesus. S. R. B. 1304; T. B. 29.

Answers to 25 Review and Test Questions on Course I, on Page 30 of Text Book

1. Genesis, Psalms, Isaiah; Matthew, John, Acts, Romans, Hebrews.
2. The book of beginnings.
3. Adam, Abraham, Isaac, Jacob, Joseph.
4. It shows man subject to the will of God, the source of all law.
5. Experience.
6. Psalms 19 and 119.

7. Psaltery, harp, trumpet, cymbals, timbrel.
8. Isaiah is the greatest of the writing prophets, and his prophecies are strongly evangelical or Messianic.
9. The destruction of 185,000 Assyrian soldiers occurred in one night.
10. Christ, as weak and rejected in the first advent; but a mighty conqueror in the second advent.
11. The Sermon on the Mount.
12. Mary the mother of Jesus, Mary Magdalene, and Mary of Bethany. S. R. B. 994.
13. The kingdom of heaven. S. R. B. 996.
14. Word, as a term for Christ.
15. "Sir, we would see Jesus" (John 12. 21).
16. As a term for the Holy Spirit.
17. The advent of the Holy Spirit.
18. His sermons at Pentecost and in the house of Cornelius.
19. Christ's commission of Paul as the chief apostle to the Gentiles, his founding of many churches, and writing of thirteen epistles.
20. Sin, redemption, justification.
21. The old or natural man and the new or spiritual man.
22. In the eighth chapter, and through the Holy Spirit.
23. Jews.
24. Christ is better than Moses, the New Covenant better than the Mosaic Covenant, the offering of Christ better than the Old Testament offerings.
25. Christ's priesthood is unchangeable, and His offering final or once for all.

Answers to Questions on Page 35 of Text Book

1. Seven.
2. Eight.
3. Dispensations have broad or general terms like Innocency, Law; covenants, those relating to place or person, as Edenic, Mosaic. Dispensations are progressive stages expressive of God's will in dealing with man; covenants are agreements between God and man to make effective God's will for these stages.
4. Partnership laws and actual partnerships agreed to under them.
5. Elohim.
6. In man's tri-unity (spirit, soul, body), and in his moral nature. S. R. B. 5.
7. By their beginning with the simple and particular and concluding with the complex and universal. T. B. 33.
8. As a preparation for his spiritual wellbeing.
9. It is God's supreme aim.
10. The disobedience and fall of our first parents.

Answers to Questions on Page 37 of Text Book

1. When mankind passes from the Dispensation of Innocency to that of Conscience.
2. The known will of God, knowledge of good and evil, personal life constantly tested.
3. Good, evil, right, wrong, conscience, virtue.
4. The faculty in man by which he distinguishes between right and wrong.
5. Our acquiring light from the Bible and other sources as to what is right and wrong.
6. The seed of the woman shall bruise the serpent's head (Gen. 3. 15).
7. There still remain parenthood, the family, the home.
8. It develops order, self-control, good habits, power of will.
9. By ignorance, selfishness, mismanagement.
10. Strength, personality, character.

Answers to Questions on Page 39 of Text Book

1. Man organized in society.
2. Government over the whole or the subordinate parts of a distinct clan, tribe, or nation. T. B. 38.
3. Capital punishment appears more likely to be retained. T. B. 38.
4. For God.
5. The confusion of tongues.
6. Israel.
7. Hamitic, Semitic, Japhetic.
8. By optimism, social aspiration, good humour, and a distinct racial creative gift in music.
9. To be the channel of divine revelation.
10. Creation of the great elements of civilization, as shown in the contributions of Greece, Rome, Germany, France, Britain, America.

Answers to Questions on Page 41 of Text Book

1. A slender rill. S. R. B. 19.
2. That it may at last purify the river itself. S. R. B. 19.
3. First the natural posterity; second, the spiritual posterity; third, the posterity through Ishmael. S. R. B. 25.
4. Twenty. T. B. 40.
5. Eighteen and a half. T. B. 40.
6. Again to have Palestine as a homeland. T. B. 40.
7. To receive and preserve the divine revelation, and to produce the Messiah. S. R. B. 19.
8. Three. S. R. B. 25.
9. The Palestinian Covenant. S. R. B. 1297.
10. "In thee shall all the families of the earth be blessed" (Gen. 12. 4). S. R. B. 25.

Answers to Questions on Page 43 of Text Book

1. When Israel rashly accepted the law (Ex. 19. 8). S. R. B. 20.
2. No. S. R. B. 20.
3. The Exodus and the Cross. S. R. B. 94.
4. The Commandments, the "judgments," and the "ordinances." S. R. B. 95.
5. The righteous will of God. S. R. B. 95.
6. The social life of Israel. S. R. B. 95.
7. Master and servant, injuries to the person, rights of property. S. R. B. 95–98.
8. The religious life of Israel. S. R. B. 95.
9. The tabernacle, priesthood, and sacrifices. T. B. 43.
10. By God's action, on the basis of the man's offering, and in anticipation of Christ's sacrifice. S. R. B. 110.

Answers to Questions on Page 45 of Text Book

1. Grace is the kindness and love of God our Saviour toward man. S. R. B. 1115.
2. Justification, redemption, grace, forgiveness. S. R. B. 1192.
3. Justification originates in grace, is through the redemptive work of Christ, and is by faith, not works. S. R. B. 1195.
4. The walk and service of the saved.
5. The ministry of such gift as he may have received. S. R. B. 1222.
6. In grace. T. B. 44.
7. First, the free gift of salvation, and then, out of a saved state, works. S. R. B. 1195.
8. They are earned by works. S. R. B. 1214.
9. Future.
10. Under law God demands righteousness from man; under grace He gives righteousness to man. Law blesses the good; grace saves the bad. S. R. B. 1115.

SUPPLEMENT—Answers to Questions

Answers to Questions on Page 47 of Text Book

1. Kingdom and the Fulness of Times. S. R. B. 1115, 1250.
2. By covenanting to build David's house, family line, or posterity. T. B. 46; S. R. B. 362.
3. Eighty-ninth. S. R. B. 643.
4. Luke 1. 32, 33.
5. Isaiah ch. 11. S. R. B. 723.
6. The time of testimony ends in judgment; the time of toil ends in rest and reward; the time of humiliation and suffering ends in glory. S. R. B. 1250.
7. Restoration to their own land and conversion. During the great tribulation a remnant out of all Israel will turn to Jesus as Messiah, and will become His witnesses after the removal of the church. S. R. B. 1205, 1206.
8. Destruction of the Gentile world system by the smiting stone. S. R. B. 901.
9. Even the animal and material creation, cursed for man's sake, will experience deliverance. S. R. B. 1198.
10. By restoring the Davidic monarchy in His own person, and establishing His power over all the earth. S. R. B. 1227.

Answers to 25 Review and Test Questions on Course II on Page 48 of Text Book

1. A dispensation is a period of time during which man is tested in respect of obedience to some *specific* revelation of the will of God. T. B. 32.
2. Human Government, Law, and Grace.
3. Partnership.
4. Testing and saving man.
5. The Edenic Covenant.
6. In harmony with each other.
7. A peaceful, charming, and fostering environment. T. B. 34
8. Goodness or virtue means a definite choice of right as over against its opposite. T. B. 36.
9. Enables us to see and obligates us to do the right. T. B. 36.
10. By overcoming obstacles we develop strength and character T. B. 37.
11. For their right working all forms of organized society need to be regulated or to have Human Government.
12. To be the channel for the divine revelation.
13. The main elements of civilization.
14. Abraham.
15. The Messiah.
16. The regaining of Palestine as a homeland.
17. Moses.
18. From the giving of the law to the death of Christ, or from Sina to Calvary. T. B. 42.
19. As an instruction in righteousness. T. B. 43.
20. The kindness and love of God toward man.
21. The New Covenant.
22. Salvation is by grace through faith, unearned by works. T. B 44, 45.
23. It is yet to come.
24. The Davidic Covenant.
25. By the angel Gabriel in announcing to Mary the birth of th Christ. T. B. 46.

Answers to Questions on Page 53 of Text Book

1. The Pentateuch.

152

2. Genesis.
3. A contrasting type of Christ. T. B. 52.
4. Of the church as the bride of Christ.
5. The mere man of the earth. Cain came by way of *works*.
6. The spiritual man. Abel came by way of *blood*.
7. The saints who will be "caught up" before the great tribulation.
8. God the Father and Christ as the Son "obedient unto death."
9. Of the nation descended from him.
10. Of Christ.

Answers to Questions on Page 55 of Text Book

1. First, of the church as a habitation of God through the Spirit; second, of the believer; third, of the things in the heavens. T. B. 54.
2. Gold, divine glory; silver, redemption; brass, judgment, as in the brazen altar and the serpent of brass.
3. Blue, heavenly in nature or origin; purple, royalty; scarlet, sacrifice.
4. From God Himself working outward toward man.
5. From the worshipper, moving toward God dwelling in the holy of holies.
6. Christ. The acacia-wood typified His humanity; the gold, His deity; the tables of the law, Christ as having God's law in His heart; manna, wilderness food of His people; Aaron's rod, Himself the resurrection. In its *use* it typified God's throne, which, by the mercy-seat sprinkled with blood, became a throne of grace and not of judgment. S. R. B. 101.
7. Christ our intercessor.
8. Christ as the Bread of God.
9. Christ our light, shining in the power of the sevenfold Spirit.
10. The Cross. The height of the altar of burnt offering shows that the atonement more than saves *us*—it glorifies God.

Answers to Questions on Page 57 of Text Book

1. After Melchisedec is the *royal authority* and unending *duration* of Christ's high priesthood. Melchisedec was a priest of the "most high God." This is the Gentile name of God. Here is a priesthood before and entirely apart from Judaism and the law, as the argument is in Hebrews (Heb. 7. 1–22). S. R. B. 23.
2. In respect to His *work*, Christ follows the Aaronic pattern. S. R. B. 23, 1295.
3. Holiness to the Lord.
4. With the names of the tribes.
5. The ephod.
6. The robe of the ephod.
7. The linen coat.
8. Bullock, sheep, goat, turtle dove, and young pigeon.
9. Judgment, condemning; manifestation of Himself, approving; purification.
10. To the offering or sacrifice made by Christ.

Answers to Questions on Page 59 of Text Book

1. That they can be used with reference to the same thing.
2. There is an emblematic or resemblance element in the type that is not always so evident in the symbol. T. B. 58.
3. To make them clearer by contrast.
4. Evil invading a world where innocence reigns.
5. Purity honoured in a realm pictured by man as ruled by carnality.
6. With the bride in the Song of Solomon.
7. Christ makes the vultures a symbol of desolation and death. Of Saint John's Gospel the true eagle has been made a symbol.
8. In one use the cross symbolizes Christ's sacrifice; in the other the believer's death to self and the world (Gal. 2. 20; 6. 14).

153

9. To the believer's final victory. Among the believer's rewards five crowns are spoken of.

10. In the book of Revelation, for Christ.

Answers to Questions on Page 61 of Text Book

1. The Bible itself.

2. It gives the opportunity to the Gentiles, and it will pass away and Israel will be saved.

3. The living believers at the time of Christ's second coming.

4. That of the Holy Spirit.

5. First, in redeeming the church; second, in sanctifying the church; third, in perfecting the church as His bride.

6. By our living Him out. This is the best proof *to the world*. The best proof is Gal. 2. 20; Col. 1. 29; etc.

7. "All the treasures of wisdom and knowledge" (Col. 2. 2, 3, 9).

8. "God was manifest in the flesh, justified in the Spirit, . . . believed on in the world, received up into glory" (1 Tim. 3. 16).

9. The beast "out of the sea"—the emperor-Beast (Rev. 13. 1-10).

10. Ephesus gives the general state of the church at the period A. D. 96; Smyrna, the period of great persecutions; Pergamos the church settled down in the world at the time of Constantine, say A. D. 316; Thyatira is the Papacy developed out of the Pergamos state; Sardis is the Protestant Reformation period; Philadelphia is whatever bears clear testimony to the Word and the Name in the period of self-satisfied profession represented by Laodicea, S. R. B. 1332.

Answers to Questions on Page 63 of Text Book

1. The Old Testament prophetic vision gave Christ's rejection and crucifixion blended with His glory.

2. It is the existing age, beginning with our Lord's personal ministry and ending with the "harvest." S. R. B. 1014.

3. Yes.

4. The parable of the Sower is foundational, and Christ Himself interprets it.

5. The alien character of some who appear to be members of the kingdom.

6. Rapid but unsubstantial growth of the kingdom.

7. The working of evil doctrine.

8. Christ is the buyer at the cost of His blood, and Israel is the treasure. S. R. B. 1017.

9. The church is the pearl of great cost.

10. The drag-net shows the kingdom tending to gather to itself what is foreign to it.

Answers to Questions on Page 65 of Text Book

1. Why do the godly suffer? Does sickness or loss mean that there is something wrong in the character or life of the one concerned?

2. They are also sifted.

3. They prove to be dogmatists. S. R. B. 571, 574–576.

4. He comes face to face with Jehovah.

5. The godly are afflicted that they may gain self-knowledge and self-judgment that will lead to greater fruitfulness. S. R. B. 597.

6. Of pure marital love. S. R. B. 705.

7. Of Christ, the Son and His heavenly Bride, the Church. S. R. B. 705.

8. The book of Revelation.

9. "Unveiling," or "revelation." S. R. B. 1212.

10. The manifestation of the man of sin, the great tribulation, the return of the Lord, the resurrections, and the judgments. S. R. B. 898.

Answers to 25 Review and Test Questions on Course III on Page 66 of Text Book

1. A divinely purposed illustration of some truth. T. B. 50.
2. A previously hidden truth, now divinely revealed, but in which a supernatural element still remains despite the revelation. T. B. 50.
3. A similitude used to teach or enforce a truth. T. B. 50.
4. Job, Song of Solomon, Daniel, Revelation. T. B. 51.
5. A type of the church as the bride of Christ. T. B. 52.
6. Of the mere man of the earth. Cain came by works.
7. Of the spiritual man. Abel came by blood.
8. Of the church, of the believer, and of the things in the heavens. S. R. B. 101.
9. Of Christ our intercessor, and of our prayers and praises ascending to God through Him. S. R. B. 110, 111.
10. Of Christ, the Bread of God, nourisher of the Christian's life as a believer-priest. S. R. B. 102.
11. In the *royal authority* and unending *duration* of His high priesthood, and of a Gentile priesthood before Judaism.
12. In respect to His *work*.
13. Of the offering of Christ.
14. There is an emblematic or resemblance element in the type, that may not appear so fully in the symbol.
15. The cross.
16. Revelation.
17. "Christ liveth in me" (Gal. 2. 20).
18. It is another proof that Christ possesses the God nature.
19. A. D. 96. S. R. B. 1331.
20. The Sower, The Grain of Mustard Seed, the Leaven, the Hid Treasure, the Pearl.
21. In an evil sense.
22. That the church is the pearl of great price.
23. As to why the godly suffer.
24. To gain self-knowledge and self-judgment leading to greater fruitfulness.
25. "Unveiling." S. R. B. 1212.

Answers to Questions on Page 71 of Text Book

1. Genesis, Exodus, Leviticus, Numbers, Deuteronomy.
2. The law, the books of Moses, or Moses.
3. Redemption.
4. In Genesis 3. 15. "It shall bruise thy head and thou shalt bruise his heel."
5. "In thee shall all the families of the earth be blessed" (Gen. 12. 3).
6. First, a divinely chosen deliverer. Second, rejected by Israel, he turns to the Gentiles. Third, during his rejection he gains a Gentile bride. Fourth, afterward he again appears as Israel's deliverer, and is accepted. Fifth, officially Moses typifies Christ as Prophet, Advocate, Intercessor, and Leader, or King. S. R. B. 72.
7. First, the lamb must be without blemish, and likewise Christ's public life was the testing of His holiness. Second, the lamb must be slain. Third, the blood must be applied. Fourth, the blood constituted a perfect protection from judgment. S. R. B. 84.
8. Type of Christ as "the bread of life," come down from heaven to die "for the life of the world." It typifies Christ in humiliation. S. R. B. 91.
9. A type of Christ in resurrection. God put life into Aaron's rod only. So all the authors of religions have died, Christ among them, but only He was raised from the dead and, exalted to be a High Priest. S. R. B. 190.
10. His return, restoration of Israel to the land, her national conversion, and judgment of her oppressors. S. R. B. 250.

Answers to Questions on Page 73 of Text Book

1. In 1 Peter 1. 10–12.
2. The Palestinian and the Davidic Covenants. S. R. B. 250, 362, 711.
3. Its Messianic character. S. R. B. 711.
4. Both suffering and glory. S. R. B. 711.
5. Isaiah, chapter 53.
6. Isaiah, chapter 11.
7. In the two advents: the first advent to redemption through suffering; the second advent to the kingdom in glory. S. R. B. 711.
8. Daniel and Jonah.
9. Nebuchadnezzar's.
10. Head of gold for Babylon; breast and arms of silver for Media-Persia; lower body of brass for Greece (under Alexander); legs of iron, and toes of iron and clay, for Rome, Eastern and Western empires, and their later divisions. Christ enters in the form of a Stone, smiting and breaking in pieces Gentile world-rule and filling the whole earth. S. R. B. 901.

Answers to Questions on Page 75 of Text Book

1. The Law, the Prophets, and the Writings.
2. First.
3. The inspired prayer-and-praise book of Israel. S. R. B. 599.
4. Five.
5. The Messianic Psalms.
6. Sixteen.
7. Psalm 2.
8. Psalm 22.
9. Psalm 45.
10. Psalm 72.

Answers to Questions on Page 77 of Text Book

1. Manifestation.
2. A divinely provided Introduction to the New Testament. S. R. B. 989.
3. Not a biography but a Personality. S. R. B. 989.
4. To cause us to see and know Him whom they reveal. S. R. B. 989.
5. Christ as covenanted King. S. R. B. 993.
6. Jesus is the personal name, Christ the official name. S. R. B. 994.
7. Jesus means "Saviour"; Christ means "The Anointed," or "Messiah."
8. Christ as Servant,—the mighty worker.
9. Christ as Man,—the human-divine One.
10. Christ as God,—the eternal word in the terms of human life.

Answers to Questions on Page 79 of Text Book

1. Propagation. T. B. 78.
2. To the Christian life and action.
3. Makes real that Christ continues to do and teach as living Leader of His kingdom. T. B. 78, 79.
4. Things pertaining to the kingdom.
5. The time is God's secret.
6. Peter.
7. The day of Pentecost.
8. The imprisonment of the apostles and the inhibition to preach. S. R. B. 1153.
9. At the martyrdom of Stephen and at the conviction and conversion of Paul.
10. In the decisive points of Paul's apostleship.

Answers to Questions on Pages 80 and 81 of Text Book

1. Explanation.
2. Probably six.
3. They come at the climax of the volume of Scripture.
4. Central and supreme.
5. Because the church is an organism, the body of Christ, instinct with His life. S. R. B. 1189.
6. "Head over all things to the church" (Eph. 1. 22).
7. He makes Christ co-equal with God in honour. T. B. 80.
8. Christ is the "chief Shepherd" (1 Pet. 5. 4).
9. "The mercy of our Lord Jesus Christ unto eternal life" (Jude 21).
10. "Only begotten Son" (1 John 4. 9).

Answers to Questions on Page 82 of Text Book

1. All the purposes of God in and through Christ are consummated. T. B. 82.
2. Consummation of the manifestation and mission of Christ. T. B. 82.
3. Consummation of the process of divine redemption. T. B. 82.
4. He is not now seated upon His own throne. S. R. B. 1334.
5. Denial of the Christian truth of the incarnation. S. R. B. 1342.
6. The Beast out of the earth and the False Prophet—two terms for the last ecclesiastical head of the forces against Christ. S. R. B. 1343.
7. The Beast out of the sea (Rev. 13. 1–8) is the last civil head of the opposing forces. S. R. B. 1343.
8. His being worthy to open the book of redemption (Rev. 5. 2–9); His overthrow of the mystical Babylon, symbolizing the Roman empire (Rev. 18. 1–19); His binding and dooming of Satan (Rev. 20. 1–10).
9. Division I—The Patmos Vision; Division II—The Church Age; Division III—The Kingdom Age. S. R. B. 1330; T. B. 83.
10. The seven sevens of Revelation are: first, the seven churches of chapters 2 and 3; second, Seals; third, Trumpets; fourth, Personages; fifth, Bowls; sixth, Dooms; seventh, New Things. S. R. B. 1330; T. B. 83.

Answers to 25 Review and Test Questions on Course IV on Page 84 of Text Book

1. The increasingly full and clear disclosure of Christ, as we advance through the Bible.
2. For Christ.
3. By a person, warm and winning.
4. The portions before the Gospels look forward to Him; those after the Gospels look backward to Him.
5. He is a divinely chosen deliverer; he is rejected, gains a Gentile bride, returns, and is accepted. Like Christ, he is prophet, intercessor, and leader.
6. The lamb must be without blemish, and to test this it was kept up four days. So Christ's public life had the testing under hostile scrutiny which proved His holiness. He, being slain and the blood being applied, is a perfect protection from judgment.
7. Aaron's rod alone received life again from God and budded. So, among the founders of religions, Christ alone was raised from the dead and His service as High Priest continued.
8. At various points it portrays the person and work of Christ.
9. Isa. 9. 6, 7; Zech. 9. 9, 10.
10. Yes. See Isa. 60. 3–10, etc.
11. Messianic Psalms.
12. Psalm 2.
13. Psalm 23.
14. Manifestation.
15. His personality.

16. In Matthew, King; in Mark, Servant; in Luke, Man; in John, God.
17. Propagation.
18. The Holy Spirit.
19. Christ.
20. Explanation.
21. The church as Christ's body.
22. By making Him co-equal with God, in his opening words (Jas. 1. 1).
23. Consummation.
24. The Beast out of the earth and the false prophet, the last ecclesiastical head, as the Beast out of the sea is the last civil head. T. B. 82.
25. By His coming in power and majesty and great glory.

Answers to Questions on Pages 88 and 89 of Text Book

1. In the kingdom of Israel.
2. When He sent out the seventy (Luke 10. 1).
3. Peter and John at Jerusalem (Acts 4. 19).
4. The two tend to strengthen and balance each other.
5. John the Baptist.
6. Ahab and Jezebel.
7. At the brook Cherith and with the widow at Zarephath.
8. Mount Carmel.
9. Mount Sinai.
10. A more quiet work of conservation.

Answers to Questions on Page 91 of Text Book

1. Athaliah. S. R. B. 941.
2. Joash. S. R. B. 930.
3. Elijah and Elisha.
4. Baal. T. B. 90.
5. From the Sidonians or Phœnicians.
6. Jezebel.
7. Spiritual Israel within national Israel. There is a believing remnant of Jews now, according to the election of grace. The remnant is composed of Jewish believers in Jesus. S. R. B. 975, 1205.
8. The people of Edom.
9. The day of the Lord, and the kingdom.
10. The outpouring of the Spirit, the return of the Lord, and full kingdom blessing. S. R. B. 930.

Answers to Questions on Page 93 of Text Book

1. At Tekoa in Judea, south of Bethlehem.
2. In Israel.
3. Jeroboam II.
4. Amaziah, priest of the calf worship at Bethel.
5. Righteousness.
6. It embraces judgment on six surrounding peoples or countries: Syria, Philistia, Phœnicia, Edom, Ammon, Moab; and on Judah and Israel.
7. Contemporary with Amos in Israel and Isaiah and Micah in Judah. S. R. B. 921.
8. *Lo-ammi*—"Not my people," and *Ammi*—"my people."
9. The Church is Christ's virgin wife and heavenly bride; Israel is Jehovah's adulterous but restored earthly wife. S. R. B. 922.
10. Loving-kindness.

Answers to Questions on Page 95 of Text Book

1. Jeroboam II.
2. They had been most cruel enemies of his people.
3. He foreshadows the Hebrew people, out of their own land, a trouble

to the Gentiles, yet witnessing to them. Also he typifies Christ as the sent one, raised from the dead, and carrying salvation to the Gentiles. S. R. B. 943.

    4.   No; but as a means of blessing all mankind. S. R. B. 19.

    5.   Yes. See S. R. B. 1137.

    6.   He started to go to one of the farthermost points in the opposite direction from Nineveh.

    7.   In the Atlantic coast lands of Spain about 2,300 miles west from Palestine.

    8.   About 700 miles.

    9.   Nineveh repented.

    10.   His gentleness and patience as the "God of all grace."

Answers to Questions on Page 97 of Text Book

    1.   Because of the wide reach and elevation of his prophecy and its evangelic character.

    2.   From Greece eastward to Persia and perhaps China, and from Assyria south to Ethiopia and southern Arabia.

    3.   Uzziah, Jotham, Ahaz, and Hezekiah.

    4.   About forty-two years.

    5.   He was a village prophet, obscure and little known, yet a kindred spirit with the powerful leader Isaiah.

    6.   The same passage found in them both (T. B. 96), and both being markedly Messianic.

    7.   In his first chapter. T. B. 96.

    8.   In his tenth chapter. T. B. 96.

    9.   The Messianic element. T. B. 97.

    10.   The remnant, the day of the Lord, and the kingdom. T. B. 97.

Answers to Questions on Page 99 of Text Book

    1.   Southwest of Jerusalem, about half way to Gaza.

    2.   Between Isaiah and Jeremiah.

    3.   Against Nineveh.

    4.   Discovery of the book of the law in the time of Josiah, and the revival that resulted. T. B. 98.

    5.   Of Josiah.

    6.   His holiness.

    7.   "The just shall live by his faith" (Hab. 2. 4).

    8.   The pre-exilic and exilic.

    9.   Anathoth and Mizpah in Judah and Tahpanhes in Egypt.

    10.   The Babylonian captivity, the return after seventy years, the world-wide dispersion, the final regathering, the kingdom-age. T. B. 99.

Answers to Questions on Page 101 of Text Book

    1.   Nahum, because both are concerned with Nineveh.

    2.   Zephaniah, because near Jeremiah in period and message.

    3.   Habakkuk, because, with Malachi, he stresses God's holiness.

    4.   They both passed from Jerusalem to Babylon and were prophets of the exile. Both are apocalyptic in type and have in view the whole house of Israel.

    5.   Symbol and vision.

    6.   Chebar.

    7.   The king's palace.

    8.   Nebuchadnezzar, Belshazzar, and Darius.

    9.   Seventy-three years. S. R. B. 898.

    10.   The whole course of Gentile world-rule to its end in catastrophe, and the setting up of the Messianic kingdom. S. R. B. 898.

Answers to Questions on Page 103 of Text Book

1. The long stretch of the Arabian desert on a straight course between the two cities.
2. Under Zerubbabel.
3. About 50,000.
4. In B. C. 520.
5. The carrying out of the rebuilding of the temple.
6. Symbolism, great Messianic passages, and warning to Gentile world-powers respecting their just treatment of Israel.
7. B. C. 458.
8. About 4,500.
9. The love of Jehovah, the sins of the priests and of the people, and the day of the Lord. S. R. B. 980.
10. B. C. 397.

Answers to 25 Review and Test Questions on Course V on Page 104 of Text Book

1. Revivalists and patriots, and, in their regular mode of working, inspired preachers. T. B. 86, 101.
2. Elijah and Elisha.
3. Rocklike strength.
4. Quiet faithfulness and firmness in conserving results.
5. Baal worship.
6. Edom.
7. "I will pour out my Spirit upon all flesh" (Joel 2. 28; Acts 2. 17).
8. The kingdom of Israel.
9. Righteousness.
10. Loving-kindness.
11. Its outreach to the Gentile world.
12. He started for the most distant point then known in the direction away from Nineveh.
13. The fear and the prospect that his own kingdom of Israel might soon be overthrown by Assyria.
14. The first and the last were Uzziah and Hezekiah.
15. China.
16. Micah.
17. Hezekiah.
18. "The just shall live by faith."
19. The kingdom of Judah was overthrown by Nebuchadnezzar, and the people went as captives to Babylon.
20. The exile.
21. Apocalyptic.
22. In Babylon.
23. God's house is neglected, and should be finished.
24. Both advents of Christ are in his prophecy. God has given the surrounding nations authority and will hold them to account.
25. B. C. 397.

Answers to Questions on Page 109 of Text Book

1. The new birth.
2. Discipline and teaching.
3. In Hosea. T. B. 108.
4. The part from Egypt to Kadesh-Barnea.
5. God's power to turn untoward things into blessing.
6. God's power to give rest and refreshment by the way.
7. That the generation that came out of Egypt doubted God's power, and did not go up from Kadesh-barnea to take possession of their promised land.

8. They express redemption, a holy walk, unity through the Holy Spirit, etc. S. R. B. 156–158.

9. Instruction in righteousness.

10. By the spiritual truths of the Word, fellowship with Him, and personal Christian experiences.

Answers to Questions on Page 111 of Text Book

1. Enlightenment and understanding, and full spiritual knowledge.
2. Stages of advance are seen in certain books of the Bible.
3. God's existence, and the final judgment.
4. Divine wisdom applied to earthly conditions.
5. The character of Christ.
6. Hebrews and the Epistles of Peter, James, and Jude.
7. Enlightened or illuminated.
8. Assurance.
9. *Gnosis*, meaning transcendent knowledge.
10. *Epignosis*, "full-knowledge," or super-knowledge.

Answers to Questions on Page 113 of Text Book

1. The revealed will of God.
2. Because it is a departure from the true path, the will of God.
3. Among Scripture aims are "reproof" and "correction" (2 Tim. 3. 16), which answer for warning.
4. The fall, and building of tower of Babel.
5. Lot and Esau.
6. Making a market of his prophetic gift. The love of money.
7. Turning away from allegiance to God to serve the gods of other peoples and take up their immoral ways.
8. Self-will, instead of obeying God.
9. Apostasy.
10. When Christians get back under law, instead of "standing fast in the liberty" of grace; struggling in their own strength at "the works of the flesh," under law, in contrast with the "the fruit of the Spirit," under grace (Gal. 5. 17–26).

Answers to Questions on Page 115 of Text Book

1. The Old Testament prayer appeals to a covenant or to God as ruler; the New Testament prayer to Him as Father.
2. The Old Testament prayer emphasizes earthly claims and awards; the New Testament, spiritual needs and bestowals.
3. The prayer of Abraham for Sodom and Gomorrah asked that the cities be spared if a certain number of righteous persons were found in them.
4. Sin judged, forgiveness and cleansing through the blood, cleansed, Spirit-filled, service, worship, zeal for Zion.
5. The filial relationship, exalting God as Father.
6. The matter concerns the divine family.
7. It comes at the beginning.
8. The kingdom is put before personal interest.
9. It is accepted beforehand.
10. Safety from the world and the evil one, and our sanctification and unity.

Answers to Questions on Page 117 of Text Book

1. Service is an essential proof of life; and Christ says: "I have chosen you, and ordained you, that ye should go and bring forth fruit" (John 15. 16).
2. Among his latest words were these: "As for me and my house, we will serve the Lord."

3. She did a beautiful service to Naomi when she remained with her, and gave another example of service when she gleaned in the harvest field.

4. Esther served the interests and continued safety of her people by putting her own life in peril.

5. As Priest He offers Himself in sacrifice; as Priest-shepherd He ever lives to make intercession. As Prophet He proclaims the name of Jehovah as Father of those who accept His Son as their Saviour. As King He fulfils the Davidic Covenant, restoring the dominion of man over creation, and of the Father over all. S. R. B. 658.

6. We see the bride satisfied with her washed feet, while the Bridegroom is toiling. Her state is not one of sin, but of neglect of service—mysticism, unbalanced by the activities of the Christian warfare. S. R. B. 707.

7. Cleansing, abiding, obedience. S. R. B. 1136.

8. The Father is glorified in us.

9. Enduing believers with spiritual gifts or enablements for a varied service; also making individual Christians themselves gifts—apostles, evangelists, pastors, teachers—bestowed on the church.

10. Christ has declared: "He that followeth me shall not walk in darkness but shall have the light of life" (John 8. 12).

Answers to Questions on Page 119 of Text Book

1. Worship and fellowship.
2. The beginning of life, and of ruin through sin.
3. Redemption.
4. Worship and communion.
5. As composed of the breast typifying affliction, and the shoulder, strength, and being, eaten by the priest it carries the idea of man's fellowship with God.
6. At the laying of the foundations of the temple.
7. Psalm 84.
8. It continues the principle that one seventh of the time is especially sacred, but makes voluntary our assembly, fellowship, and worship.
9. A new and living way of approach to God opened to all believers by the shed blood of Christ.
10. To walk in the light is to live in fellowship with the Father and the Son.

Answers to Questions on Page 121 of Text Book

1. His walk with God.
2. The Friend of God.
3. At Peniel when the angel wrestled with Jacob and "touched the hollow of his thigh," and Jacob became a cripple in his self-strength.
4. To be shown the glory of God.
5. To be like God in character.
6. Because he faced for years intense opposition by leaders and people.
7. "There is none upon earth that I desire beside thee" (Psa. 73. 25); "I meditate on thee in the night watches" (Psa. 63. 6).
8. Their knowledge of and nearness to God.
9. No sin between the soul and Him; all wisdom, life, and strength derived from Him; fellowship, communion. S. R. B. 1136, 1137.
10. The one Spirit-baptism seals the believer for God; but there may be many Spirit-fillings. S. R. B. 1149.

Answers to 25 Review and Test Questions on Course VI on Page 122 of Text Book

1. The personal factor or personality is seen in God and in His image stamped on man—in man's soul and self-consciousness.

2. Enoch and Noah, Gideon and Deborah, David and Hezekiah, Jeremiah and Malachi.

3. Because Christianity is built about Him.

4. The Psalms, the prophets, Christ, and the New Testament writers deal more and more with the inward life.

5. Understanding and practice of that which is good cannot be handed down to young life; they must be inculcated in each new generation.

6. The part from the Israelites leaving Egypt to their encamping at Kadesh-barnea.

7. Their experiences during the exodus, the giving of the law at Sinai, and the teaching influence of the great festivals.

8. Ecclesiastes, Proverbs, and the prophetical books.

9. "Enlightenment" and "Assurance" for the individual Christian go far beyond what the Old Testament believer possessed.

10. Because he has the unction and teaching of the Holy Spirit (1 John 2. 20, 27).

11. Because sin has made us liable to worldliness, error of judgment, and moral and spiritual temptation.

12. Saul (1 Sam. 15. 22, 23); Jeroboam (1 Kings 14. 15, 16).

13. When Christians get back under law, instead of "standing fast in the liberty" of grace; struggling in their own strength at "the works of the flesh," under law, in contrast with "the fruit of the Spirit," under grace (Gal. 5. 17-26).

14. Because it embodies the seven essential steps of a saved man passing through the gospel experience of restoration to fellowship. T. B. 114.

15. Yes; the two operations of God cohere in relations as Creator and Father.

16. The Lord's Prayer teaches that prayer rests on the filial relationship, and is a child's petition to an all-wise, loving, powerful, Father-God. Prayer begins with worship; puts the interests of the kingdom first; and accepts beforehand the Father's will.

17. As shown by his farewell declaration, he and his house will serve the Lord.

18. Yes.

19. That they may perform their proper function, and faithfully minister.

20. It serves these ends, but in a more full and voluntary manner.

21. The rent veil signifies new access to God on the part of all believers by the shed blood of Christ.

22. It interrupts and prevents it.

23. Complete fellowship with God.

24. "I remember thee upon my bed, and meditate on thee in the night watches."

25. To abide in Christ means to have no sin unjudged, no interest apart from Him; also to take all burdens to Him, and draw all strength from Him.

Answers to Questions on Page 127 of Text Book

1. The self-existent One.

2. The self-existent One who reveals Himself—the redemptive name of God.

3. By the plural name, Elohim, by use of plural pronouns, and by the threefold ascription, "Holy, holy, holy" (Isa. 6. 3, 8).

4. At the baptism of Christ. The Spirit descends upon the Son, and at the same moment the Father's voice is heard from heaven.

5. At the point of man's creation.

6. As Distributor of the earth. This is the Gentile designation of God.

7. He sought the sinning ones and clothed them with coats of skins—expressive of sacrifice.
8. His holiness.
9. His hatred and judgment of sin.
10. His love for and redemption of sinners.

Answers to Questions on Page 129 of Text Book

1. The creation of the heavens and the earth, and the creation of animal life.
2. In man's tri-unity—spirit, soul, and body—and in his moral nature.
3. "Soul" in man implies self-conscious life, and a vaster content than in the animal.
4. The fact that they are divisible (Heb. 4. 12), and that the body in burial is a natural body (literally "soul-body") and in resurrection a spiritual body.
5. Affections, desires, emotions, the will, the self, and self-consciousness.
6. The power to know, to be God-conscious, and to have communication with God.
7. The body is the seat of the senses, and through these the spirit and soul have world-consciousness.
8. The temptation of Satan, leading to man's first sin.
9. "They are all gone aside, . . . there is none that doeth good, no not one" (Psa. 14. 3).
10. "Evil thoughts, adulteries, thefts, covetousness, deceit, blasphemy, pride" (Mark 7. 21, 22).

Answers to Questions on Page 131 of Text Book

1. When Lucifer in an attitude of revolt against God Himself said, "I will," sin began. S. R. B. 726.
2. The form of a serpent.
3. Transgression, iniquity, error, trespass.
4. An overstepping of the law.
5. An act inherently wrong, whether expressly forbidden or not.
6. A departure from right.
7. The intrusion of self-will into the sphere of divine authority.
8. It was and is universal, Christ alone excepted.
9. Spiritual and physical death.
10. The sacrificial death of Christ availed of by faith. S. R. B. 1194.

Answers to Quesions on Page 133 of Text Book

1. His name, "Immanuel," "God with us," and His virgin birth.
2. The Jehovah name of God, implying eternal existence, and Christ appropriated to Himself this very name, as revealed in the third chapter of Exodus. He does this throughout the Gospel according to John, which speaks of Christ's deity.
3. In such miracles as stilling the tempest and raising Lazarus.
4. In such acts as feeding the five thousand.
5. To Adam.
6. The sinlessness of Him who bore our sins. S. R. B. 147.
7. Because the sinless God-man gave His life when His blood was shed.
8. His blood upon the *altar* is efficacious, not the influence of His life. S. R. B. 150.
9. No.
10. The treating right God's holy law, so that He can righteously show mercy and put first God's public justice. The sacrifice of Christ satisfied this. S. R. B. 1195.

Answers to Questions on Page 135 of Text Book

1. At the point where Christ's sacrificial offering for mankind is complete. T. B. 134.
2. The goodness of God uplifting him by grace in Christ.
3. To be eased or comforted.
4. Change of mind, with reversal of moral attitude.
5. Of sin, of God, and of self.
6. Personal trust, apart from meritorious works, in the Lord Jesus Christ.
7. Confidence in God, that "if we ask anything according to his will, he heareth us" (1 John 5. 14, 15).
8. The believer gets a new nature, "which after God is created in righteousness and true holiness" (Eph. 4. 24).
9. Law is partial, weak, and inadequate; grace is marvelous, divine, and sufficient. Law condemns. Law condemns the best man, and grace saves the worst man. Law demands; grace gives.
10. It calls for the new birth through which the believer becomes a partaker of the divine nature.

Answers to Questions on Page 137 of Text Book

1. We have the purpose of the Father, the love of Christ, the depths and heights of redeeming grace, and the unmeasured energies of the Holy Spirit.
2. In kindness, not sinlessness.
3. By Christ's redemption and our faith.
4. Divine love, wrought into the renewed heart, outflows as the "law of liberty."
5. Love, joy, peace.
6. Longsuffering, gentleness, goodness.
7. Faith, meekness, temperance.
8. The natural man is man unrenewed through the new birth. The carnal man is the renewed man who, walking "after the flesh," remains a babe. The spiritual man is the renewed man as Spirit-filled and walking in the Spirit in full communion with God.
9. First, his own living body; second, praise to God; third, his substance.
10. Justification, as position, is the judicial act of God whereby he justly declares righteous one who believes in Jesus. As experience, it marks the believer's life when, through the indwelling Spirit, the righteousness of the law is fulfilled in him. Sanctification, as position, sets believers eternally apart for God by redemption, so that they are "saints" and "holy" from the moment of believing. As experience, the believer is being sanctified by the work of the Holy Spirit through the Scriptures, while his complete sanctification awaits the appearing of the Lord. S. R. B. 1196, 1211, 1245, 1353.

Answers to Questions on Page 139 of Text Book

1. An assembly of called-out ones.
2. That God through Peter had visited the Gentiles "to take out of them a people for his name" (Acts 15. 14).
3. Gentiles.
4. The believing (Christian) Jews.
5. Matthew 16. 18.
6. Through Paul.
7. Rome, Corinth, Galatia, Ephesus, Philippi, Colosse, and Thessalonica. S. R. B. 1189.
8. As Christ's body, and as Christ's bride.
9. The true church is the whole number of regenerate persons from Pentecost to the first resurrection. The professing church is that visible

body of professed believers existing under many names and divisions based on differences in doctrine and government. S. R. B. 1304, 1276.

10. All moral intelligences willingly subject to the will of God, whether angels, the church, or saints of past or future dispensations. It is universal and of kindred nature to the true church. S. R. B. 1003.

Answers to Questions on Page 142 of Text Book

1. He suspended the reading of Isaiah 61. 2 at the point where the gracious aspect of the first advent was covered, and did not read the latter part of the verse in which the vengeance aspect of the second advent appears.

2. As first in the series of events that mark His return.

3. Three and a half years of unexampled trouble, caused by the "beast" or evil leader known as the "man of sin."

4. God, and especially the believing Jewish remnant.

5. From the ancient hill and valley of Megiddo, southeast of Mount Carmel.

6. It marks the overthrow of the world-powers by Christ at His return.

7. From the return of Christ, on through the millennium, and other events, to the purgation of the heavens and the earth by fire. S. R. B. 1349.

8. The Kingdom of Heaven or the Kingdom-age embraces the whole period from the return of Christ the King in glory till at the end of time He delivers up the kingdom to the Father. Then the kingdom of heaven merges into the kingdom of God. S. R. B. 1003, 1341.

9. The millennium is the central and main era of a thousand years in the kingdom-age, free from conflicts and other disturbing events, and constituting the ideal rulership of Christ on earth. However, although "there is triumph over death at the first resurrection, death, 'the last enemy,' is not *destroyed* till the end of the millennium." S. R. B. 977, 1017.

10. The revolt, defeat, and judgment of Satan; the raising and judging of the wicked; the purging of the earth by fire; the delivering up of the kingdom to the Father; the ending of time and beginning of eternity; the securing of the eternal blessedness of all who believe.

Answers to 25 Review and Test Questions on Course VII on Pages 142, 143 of Text Book

1. This movement of Christian doctrine, out from and back to God, is found again and again in the scriptural order and in man's arrangement and treatment of doctrine.

2. His name, Jehovah, signifies the self-existent One who reveals Himself.

3. Perfect moral and spiritual accord constitutes the unity, and the Father, the Son, and the Holy Spirit constitute the Trinity of God.

4. As redeeming His people out of Egypt He makes the first distinct revelation of Himself by His name Jehovah. He also emphasizes His attributes as brought into exercise by redemption.

5. Body, soul, spirit.

6. Soul makes man self-conscious; spirit, God-conscious.

7. The experience and conscience of man ever confirming the statement of Scripture that all have sinned.

8. It tells of Lucifer, "son of the morning," whose intrusion of self-will into the sphere of divine authority marks the origin of sin (Isa. 14. 13, 14).

9. Going contrary to the will of God.

10. Physical and spiritual death.

11. Christ asserted His identity with the Father, and appropriated to Himself, as recorded in the Gospel of John, repeatedly the very name of Jehovah as the great I AM, as revealed in the third chapter of Exodus; and

the New Testament writers ascribe to Him divine titles, attributes, and works.

12. Luke.

13. In Christ's life of inconceivable value, as the God-man, sacrificed, and His blood placed upon the altar.

14. Reversal of one's course or moral attitude.

15. In personal trust in Christ alone.

16. Conversion shows how superior is grace to law; and its call for the new birth reveals its supernatural character.

17. Love, chief grace in our inward state; goodness, in our bearing toward man; faith in our attitude toward God.

18. Gifts are good, but only if ministered in love; benevolence is good, but not apart from love. Love is greater than knowledge, faith, and hope.

19. Divine acceptance determines position or standing; divine enablement, through the Holy Spirit, makes the given state real in experience.

20. A company or assembly of called-out ones.

21. Romans, Galatians, Ephesians, Philippians, Colossians.

22. Christ's bride (Eph. 5. 25; Rev. 21. 9).

23. It is an event, not a process, and is personal and corporeal. S. R. B. 1148.

24. Christ is Priest-King in the millennium (S. R. B. 968), and comes to take His own throne (S. R. B. 970), in Jerusalem, as capital of a kingdom established first over regathered, restored, and converted Israel, then to become universal, over the whole earth. The kingdom is one of righteousness and peace, the enormous majority of earth's inhabitants will be saved, and great heights of spiritual, intellectual, and physical perfection will be attained. S. R. B. 977, 1298.

25. In the present answer to this question the final judgment can receive careful statement. The subjects are the wicked dead, as the redeemed were raised one thousand years before. As there are degrees in punishment, the wicked are judged according to their works; with their judgment the history of the present earth ends. S. R. B. 1351. The eternal life of the redeemed which constitutes their immeasurable future is the life of God imparted in the new birth, and is an unsevered part of the life which eternally was, and eternally is, in Christ Jesus. S. R. B. 1353.

Answers to 50 Review and Test Questions on A Year's Bible Course on Pages 143, 144 of Text Book

1. To afford a sufficient variety to meet the needs of all groups and classes. T. B. 7.

2. "Balanced and two-hemisphered" means that each of the seven sub-courses shows balance in its relations with the two spheres of the Old and New Testaments. T. B. 8.

3. The salvation and upbuilding of souls through the blood of Jesus Christ. T. B. 10.

4. Because it is the foundation with which all future right development must start. T. B. 15.

5. To be in God's favour means close relation with Him, satisfaction, rest, blessedness.

6. Because it was a continuing prophecy addressed to the Davidic family giving assurance that the Messiah would enter the world through virgin birth along their line of descent. T. B. 18.

7. Declaring the *principles* of the kingdom. Jesus at once disclosed His sense of the new and supreme value which He gave to personality, character, and individuality, by carrying the quality of each act and emotion back to the innermost motive.

8. "I and my Father are one" (John 10. 30).

9. In the second division of Acts (10. 1–28. 31) Paul is prominent. a new center is established at Antioch, and the ministry is chiefly to Gentiles. S. R. B. 1147.

10. Because it embodies in the fullest way the doctrines of grace in relation to salvation. S. R. B. 1191.

11. Similitude, image, pattern, figure. T. B. 28.

12. The race at that stage was in a condition resembling the infantile state of the individual, to which attaches innocence.

13. Their sense that they were naked, and their hiding themselves from the presence of the Lord (Gen. 3. 7, 8).

14. Human government is necessary to maintain the right balance between the claims of the individual and of organized society, and to regulate the conflicting desires of individuals.

15. Because divine promise inspires and makes fruitful the interrelation of man with God, it is a proper beginning of religion.

16. While man vainly tries to win merit by obedience to law, he finds that grace is a final solution of his religious needs because it ministers salvation and assurance on the one condition of faith.

17. Because grace, meaning God's free gift according to man's need, guarantees him power to fulfil his side of the promise.

18. For the Jewish people it means restoration to Palestine and conversion to the Christian faith; for the Gentile world-system destruction by the smiting stone. Christ's new creation is given moral unity with God, and even the animal and material world experiences deliverance.

19. It appears as if the Spirit chose for the guidance of coming ages characters that had this simple teaching or typical quality.

20. Because they typify or express the union of deity and humanity in Christ.

21. Fire is a symbol of God's holiness; and is effectual for what He condemns, what He approves, and for purification.

22. For Christ the cross symbolizes sacrifice, the crown, eternal glory; for the believer cross and crown symbolize struggle and victory.

23. Because the word in the Bible has not the ordinary meaning, but signifies truths only in part revealed.

24. Taken together there is a completeness about the number as giving the result of the reactions of the Gospel in this existing age.

25. Because spiritual things "are spiritually discerned" (1 Cor. 2. 14).

26. There is a Messianic element in the Old Testament, growing more pronounced and definite as we approach the New Testament.

27. To make clear His Personality.

28. The author is Luke; and, as in his Gospel he tells what Jesus "began both to do and teach," so in Acts he shows what Jesus continued to do and teach through his Holy Spirit.

29. The Epistles of Paul and the Jewish-Christian Epistles.

30. In Revelation all the purposes of God in and through Christ are consummated.

31. Elisha represents teaching, and Elijah, action.

32. In the kingdom of Judah.

33. The kingdom of Israel.

34. Assyria, especially Nineveh its capital.

35. Isaiah prophesied in Jerusalem, and had a wide outlook on the national movements of his time; while Micah was a prophet in Moresheth-gath, a village twenty miles to the southwest.

36. In Jerusalem.

37. Daniel in Babylon and Ezekiel at Telabib, on a canal not far away.

38. The province of Judah.

39. Training and teaching.

40. Prayer and service.

41. Leviticus is the book in the Pentateuch especially marked by communion and worship. There is seen the revived spirit of fellowship and worship in Ezra (Ezra 3. 10-12). At many places in the Psalms the theme finds expression.

42. Enoch and Abraham, Jacob and Moses, Elijah and Jeremiah, the remnant.

43. With God.

44. Man.

45. Sin.

46. Christ.

47. Uplifted by grace, the soul turns to God in repentance and is converted.

48. Christian character and graces; love become supreme; and "the heavenlies," or becoming identified with Christ in nature, life, and celestial glory.

49. The "called-out" ones forming the church, Christ's body, Christ's bride; the kingdom of God.

50. Christ's return; the kingdom of heaven, kingdom-age, or millennium; future or eternal blessedness.